The Replanted Church

Rick Lawrenson

Rick Lawrenson

DEDICATION

To pastors and their churches, not yet ready to throw in the towel,
who desire God to breathe new life into their congregations
and are willing to do whatever it takes..

*Now to Him who is able to do above and beyond all that we ask
or think — according to the power that works in you—
to Him be glory in the church and in Christ Jesus to all generations,
forever and ever. Amen.*
Ephesians 3:20-21

THE REPLANTED CHURCH

Acknowledgements

Dave and Amanda, who lent me their mountain cabin for three weeks to get this done.

Jenny Wilson, who edited and corrected the manuscript.

Gail, my wife, who has been with me the entire journey.

Gordon Luff, who taught me leadership principles that I still remember decades later.

My Nags Head Church family. Without them there is no story!

INTRODUCTION

(A little context before you begin...)

A group of believers wanted to start a new church in this little resort town. New churches, like anything else new – new car, new job, new baby – bring with them a level of excitement and a chance to, if they're willing, do things differently.

At age 31, I was searching for something new myself – a new position in ministry. It was "time" (if you know what I mean) to leave the church in Virginia where I was pulling double duty as youth and music pastor. My passions and giftedness seemed to be headed more toward being the "lead pastor" of a church (I had not heard that term before in 1986, but I didn't care for the term "senior pastor") where I could preach and teach adults as well as youth.

One of my friends in ministry, the planting pastor of a rapidly growing church, hooked me up with this little group, and before long, we were off – planting a new church. My family and I moved 75 miles south. I got a couple part-time jobs and found financial support from a church-planting fellowship at my alma mater. We found a location to meet in a motel, came up with a name and a very cool logo. In addition to Sundays, we met on Wednesday nights for Bible study. Quickly, this upstart congregation grew from a handful to nearly 50 people gathering on Sundays.

Within four months of our launch, we "chartered" as a bona fide church with our own bylaws and membership. We had our first baptism and communion together. The newspaper carried our story. There was even talk of another local church (which we had outgrown already) being willing to talk of a merger.

Then, without warning (at least to my naïve receptors), the bottom fell out. The core group of people that initially "courted" me to come and start a church weren't really interested in a new church to reach the unchurched. They were disgruntled members of existing churches who didn't like their pastors or church leaders for whatever reasons. Mostly, I found, it was about control. And as always happens, that baggage - that attitude of distrust toward pastors - came with them. In less than six months, I found out I was just the newest pastor in the bull's eye of their target. I caved in to their pressure, and not wanting to do damage to the work God had begun (remember, I was naïve), I resigned.

Suddenly, I was no longer a church-planting pastor. I was crushed and awash in a sense of, "God, I have no idea what just happened. I thought You were in this, but I must have been wrong." But one thing I knew: I'd tried church planting and failed. There was no way I would go in that direction again.

The next four years found me working outside of my element in the construction trade to support my family and wondering if I'd ever be useful in a pastorate again. I was learning valuable life lessons but felt very much as though my ministry wheels were spinning in the sandy soil of the beach where we live.

The current church culture in the United States indicates that new church plants are the new wave. Towns, cities and rural settings are full of tired, old churches where the life has fizzled out long ago. So, the planting movement is exploding. As a church planter friend told me long ago, "It's easier to give birth than to raise the dead!"

Maybe. Depends on your gifting, calling and God's plan.

We are the servants of the God of heaven and earth and are rebuilding the temple
that was built many years ago, which a great king of Israel built and finished.
Ezra 5:11

Sometimes, the answer to reaching a community is not to plant a new church, but to replant the old. Not all of us are called to plant new churches. Some of us are called to lead dwindling or even comatose churches back to vitality. Unless "Ichabod" has truly been written over the door of the church, there may still be the opportunity, should God will it, for spiritual and visional CPR to bring life back.

Replanting is not for the faint of heart. Because it's not new, it doesn't pack the wow factor. Old reputations are difficult to change in the community. Antiquated church buildings aren't nearly as fun as going to church in movie theaters and motel banquet rooms. Dyed in the wool traditions that don't work aren't easily forsaken. But, it can happen!

Fast-forward twenty-seven years. Unless you knew the story, it would appear that a completely different church occupies the corner lot. Actually, that's not a totally incorrect assessment. We believe God has done something remarkable!

Without a strategic replanting, none of that would have happened. Had there not been a continual revival and transformation, most likely the church would have folded within the decade.

I'm still learning from all this. But if you are considering a replant, I'd love to share with you some of what God has already taught us here.

FOREWORD

Before we can know what it is we are supposed to do and become, we need to know who we are. If we are unable to define "church" and have a grasp on what it means to be in community with other believers and for what purposes, we cannot possibly *be* the church.

I don't have any research to back this up, other than what I've seen and heard over the years, but experience tells me most members of Bible-believing evangelical churches could not outline their own ecclesiology with, or without, chapter and verse. So, if we don't know why the church is a living organism, how in the world can we know when its vital signs are growing weak?

Let me take it a step further. further. If you know and really believe what the Bible says about the church, you'll do anything within your power to defend and sustain her. You won't sit idly by and watch her fall to sleep or worse, into a coma.

My pulpit responsibilities when I became interim pastor of Nags Head Baptist Church included the preaching on Sunday mornings and Sunday nights, as well as leading the Wednesday night prayer meeting. Because I'm one of those "Bible thumpers" – an evangelical in the true sense - I am "stronger than horseradish" (as my old Kansas raised pastor used to say) about the absolute necessity that we find our direction from the Scriptures. Replanting requires rediscovering – maybe even uncovering for some – ecclesiastical doctrine and making it plain for all who will understand.

So, on Sunday mornings, we went to Paul's epistle to the Galatians, mostly because my Galatians class in seminary was so good and the prof drilled it into our hearts and minds. It covers salvation, grace and their antithesis, legalism, so very well. But, on Sunday evenings, when my audience was more the committed in the church than the contented and the occasional guest, I went to task on teaching about the church. Not our church, so much, but God's church. That is because our church doesn't necessarily resemble His.

Taking the 11th through the 16th verses of the fourth chapter of Ephesians, our first Sunday evening series was titled "God's Work God's Way". I still rememberthat series and frequently used the title phrase in reminding them what we were to be about. It's such a rich passage that, in a nutshell, explains the beauty of a church growing, serving and being the body of Christ.

The concept of pastors *equipping* church partners so *they* could do the ministry raised an eyebrow or two. For how many generations have churches assumed that you "hired" a pastor so he could do the ministry? After all, he is called the "minister".

They were taught we are joined together to build one another up in faith and love. That means more than not tearing each other down; it includes intentionally finding ways to inspire others to Christ-likeness. Then, the word pictures Paul paints of maturation, unity and the body working together began to clarify just how important knowing who we were was to who we would become.

These truths were, to many, new nuggets. There is much more to proclaim to the church especially than evangelism Sunday after Sunday. Eyes were being opened to see what Jesus intended the living church to become. But, these were spiritual eyes, as well as ears coupled with, for the most part, receptive hearts. And what began as nuggets became foundation stones for the radical changes God would do in the years ahead.

God said to Israel through the prophet Hosea, *My people are destroyed for lack of knowledge.*[1] So, for the church to be what God intends, they must have knowledge from God on who they are and who they should be. Then, after that foundation is laid, they may be able to rise up and be. There are no shortcuts. Clever slogans and pep talks will provide light like sparklers on the 4th of July, but God wants us to be more. He ordained and created the church to be a shining city upon a hill.[2]

I believe there are many churches, perhaps plateaued or even in decline for years, who can experience renewal and new life. True, many congregations won't see turn-around because they either don't want it or refuse to believe change can be wrought. But I know for some, that kind of revival can be more than a dream. It can be reality.

---

[1] Hosea 4:6
[2] Matthew 5:14-16

Chapter 1
HOW DID THIS HAPPEN?

Let me start with the four years that preceded my becoming the pastor of Nags Head Church...

Every real leader, and that should include pastors, whether replanters or not, has worked out in his/her head a picture of what the business, team or church should look like. Call it "vision" if you want; we all have our ideals. Even when I was out of vocational ministry for four years, I was still dreaming of "one day" (if God ever allowed me to pastor again). If the leaders don't have the dream, vision or philosophy/strategy in mind, no one will. There will be no one to follow.

Whether I was pounding nails by day or behind the desk of a motel office checking in guests at night, I was thinking "church" during my four year "wilderness wandering". When your calling, gifting and education has all been on one track, and you find yourself out of necessity for survival on another track, your thoughts are perhaps too frequently introspective.

"What would I have done differently?" was the biggest question following my failure as a planter. In the summer of 1986, we moved to Nags Head to plant a new church. My relationship with those 40 or so people lasted a quick six months. Thirty years later, I still ask those same questions, although most of them have been answered. The experience formed a discontent within me that will likely never leave and will drive me to not repeat the same errors.

Those four years of exile were the most frustrating and painful of my life. Not only did I feel like a failure, but, to tell the truth, the invitations to "candidate" at churches seeking my skills weren't exactly pouring in. And it seemed the few that did come in were from dysfunctional churches looking for another short-term pastor to chew on for a while, then discard like some 7th grade romance. However, because of God's graciousness and patience, I was able to continue practicing my gifts and keeping my "tools" from becoming too rusty.

Almost teasingly, God provided me occasions to use my gifts. Frequently, the pastor of the little church in town – the one that had considered a merger with the plant - gave me opportunities to fill in for him. Every pastor, especially in small churches, wants to know that there's a go-to guy ready and able in a pinch. I was that guy and grateful to be. He was gracious in giving me many opportunities to teach.

A group of "Word-hungry" mostly seniors from various area churches invited me to teach a non-denominational weekly Bible study. Every Tuesday night for 2 years I came ready with a Bible lesson, and they came ready to learn. The encouragement to my soul was like a tall glass of southern sweet tea on a July evening.

Eventually, my wife and I joined a church pastored by a friend that required an hour and a half trek each Sunday with our three little ones. There, I became their volunteer song leader and was given the occasional opportunity to preach. Together, these three humanly unconnected ventures kept me both engaged in ministry and hungry for more.

But, even though I was ready (in my mind) and available to get back into a church staff position, nothing seemed to come together. No doors to leave the area were opening. And frankly, my previous experiences had made me less open to possibilities. I finally came to grips with the reality that I might never again vocationally lead a church. But, I questioned God every day. The passion of the calling had not left. After four years, I surrendered to the Lord with the acceptance that if I never pastored again, that was OK if that was His will.

God used a young woman who had sat under my teaching to speak a "prophetic" word to me. At least, that's how it seemed to me. (Don't let that scare you off.) She simply said, "Maybe God's not finished with you here yet." While everything pointed to the contrary - I was unhappy, unfulfilled and working like a dog doing something I didn't enjoy to make ends meet – apparently, she was right. Maybe she wasn't a prophetess...just a woman with some wisdom or simply the gift of encouragement. But her words at the time both gave me hope and frustrated me at the same time. "If that's so, then what's the hold-up?"

Four years and one month after I resigned from the church plant, God brought me into the pastorate of that little old church in the same resort town. Their bi-vocational pastor was growing older and in increasingly poor health. During those four years, he had invited me often to fill in for him on Sundays. So, I had developed a relationship with the congregation. They became used to my preaching style, and although it was different from what they were used to, they accepted it. Some even liked it!

The pastor got an idea to keep me around. Physically, he wasn't able to devote the energy it took to continue. He had been through some major church political battles during his tenure and was just tired of it. I think he knew it was time for a change. So, he made an attempt to get the church to call me as their "associate" pastor. The sixteen members who showed up for the meeting voted favorably. Well, sort of favorably. Nine voted "Aye" and seven voted "Nay". I don't know the nay's reasons. But really, does such a small church need an "associate" pastor?

He was enthusiastic when he called me that night to tell me they had "extended a call". Really? "What was the vote?" I asked. "Nine to seven. And that's a majority – enough to call you." Well, I already had a problem with the whole "majority rules democracy" application to church polity, and knowing that if that many people – nearly half - didn't want me I would likely find myself looking over my shoulder all the time, I respectfully declined the "call". I was desperate, but not that desperate. I wasn't looking to be the source of another church fight and split.

Still, he was persistent. He continued to ask me to fill the pulpit for him, letting me know that one day he was going to retire. Eventually, after hearing this for four years, I met with him and said, "Look. Either do it or don't". To my surprise, he agreed the time had come.

He announced to the church he was going to take a medical leave of absence for six months, and he may not come back. Then, in the next breath, he proposed the church vote then and there to call me as their interim pastor. It wasn't unanimous, but vote they did and with a greater majority than before. Still, I had to ask if this was what God wanted me to do. Was this what I really envisioned? Better question: would I be attempting the impossible? Honestly, while I'm certain it had been done, I didn't personally know anyone who had taken a dying, traditional, old church and saw it turn around and make a comeback. And my leadership failures of the past were always there to remind me.

The reasons why it wouldn't work outnumbered the reasons why it could. But isn't that more often than not how God-sized changes are birthed? We can weigh the pros vs. the cons, but ultimately, we must come to the conclusion the only way for it to fly is if God provides the wings.

Gail and I both wondered aloud to each other as we talked. Why would we want to go to a church barely hanging on to life? We had three children under the age of ten and there was nothing at this church but a now-you-see-it-now-you-don't Sunday school class for the kids. If the teacher didn't show up, there was no class. And besides, we really enjoyed the church we belonged to despite the long drive each Sunday. And the pastors there had told me they were going to ask me to become an elder in the church. They were men my age. Our kids loved their children's ministry. And for the time, their music was increasingly contemporary.

In 1991, Nags Head Baptist Church remained, in virtually every way, exactly as it had been in the post-war era when it was planted. All the traditions were the same. Nothing new. Sure, there had been some cosmetic changes. The pews were padded, and central air and stained glass windows had been added in the 80's. Aluminum siding now covered the asbestos shingles; a tiny foyer with new steps and a ramp had been built. But the membership, except for one young family with two little girls, all remembered the 1950's as "the good old days".

Active membership consisted of about twenty-five. Most of them were collecting Social Security. The two deacons were octogenarians whose sole ministry was to collect and count the Sunday offering, which they did on the top of the organ immediately after the last "Amen". Nothing about the church, from the dilapidated sign out front to the organ music inside, said, "Young families welcome here". Qualities such as relevance and excellence were not evident. They were simply hanging on.

The generation gap between the potential new pastor and congregants was obvious. Gail and I were in our mid-thirties. Closest to us in age was one couple ten years older and another couple, the ones with the kids, ten years younger. As I stood in the pulpit, I was looking at my parents' and grandparents' generations. The one family that was younger than us had become our friends, which was a good thing. Even the pastor and his wife need fellowship.

Nearly every day for the previous four years, I had driven by that little church on my way to and from work. Were it not for the handful of cars in the parking lot on Sundays and Wednesday nights, the appearance was lifeless. So many times, I had often asked God if a thriving congregation couldn't come from one barely holding on to life church on that corner. I actually dreamed of what it might take from a leadership perspective to bring it about.

The demographics showed great potential. Our community was rapidly growing. New schools were being built to handle the influx of new families. The combination of a booming tourist economy and the services needed brought in young adults looking for jobs. You couldn't step outside anywhere without hearing saws and hammers as homes were being built everywhere. Jobs were plenteous. A dying church sat during a thriving community. God let me see the potential.

For me, there was a polity issue as well. After my planting experience, and the ability in that experience of a few malcontents with sand spurs in their flip-flops to make my life miserable to the point of quitting, I had sworn off Baptist churches. You know how it is. "I will never again...". That was me. I must confess I was scarred with a little bitterness. But, if God was in this, then somehow, He would work out my misgivings.

I prayed. I talked to my pastor for his advice. And when the vote was cast, and the church asked me to come, I had a hard time saying "No", either to them or to God. Both Gail and I questioned the call. One hundred percent sure we were not. We must have been willing to take the risk.

A life of faith without risks doesn't exist. Faith involves the "unseen" and the "hoped for"[3], not necessarily the guaranteed. And, doubts only serve to strengthen faith. "Lord, I believe, help my unbelief"[4]. He would.

---

[3] Hebrews 11:1

[4] Mark 9:24

Up front, I also knew just maintaining the status quo was unacceptable to me and would only prolong the inevitable death of this congregation. If God truly was calling me to this church, it had to be because of the dreams and vision He had instilled in me during those four hungry years to see a church become powerful in its witness and relevant in its ministry and outreach.

My only choice was to view it as a "replant" – to take the life that existed and carefully, over time, nurture it back to health. But this wasn't mine alone to do! Fortunately, there was a tiny core within the church that ached for their church to come to life. And this new, young pastor gave them hope for God to bring that about.

One of my favorite memories was the Sunday night in January, the week before my first Sunday in the pulpit as interim pastor. That morning, we said goodbyes to our church in Virginia and headed back home so we could be in the service in Nags Head Sunday night. At the end of the service, we stood before the church to be voted in as members. As they filed by to welcome us, one of the senior ladies - a pastor's daughter herself in her late 70's who was known for speaking her mind – said to me, "I didn't vote for you to come. But now that you're here, whatever you need me to do, I'll do".

Her words represented the cooperative spirit that was necessary. I really don't think she had any inkling of what would transpire over the next few years, but she kept her word and became one of my most staunch supporters in some of the controversies that popped up. (You didn't think controversy would stay away, did you?) Years later, as I preached her funeral, tears came to my eyes as I remembered her frank but sincere and unwavering commitment to the church.

Had the whole congregation been against change, the replant would have been quickly doomed. That's not to say that there wasn't opposition! But, even those hoping for new life had to be willing to take some risks and exercise faith.

Replanting isn't all about the replanter. If church is about a person, that Person must be Christ. The real changes that would come would have made no difference at all had not the Lord of the church been preeminent.

It has to be God's desire to bring a church out of its slumber. No doubt, there are many churches that long ago lost their voice in the world. They have become social clubs or holy huddles, content to remain the same forever. As one elder lady in our church said in a business meeting when someone mentioned the need to reach more people, "I like it just like we are". That sentiment of comfort had to be changed.

It also requires people. A church plant essentially starts with a planter and a seed and builds from there. A church replant starts with a congregation, in need of new vision, new leadership...maybe new everything. But, it begins with people who need change, whether or not they know they need it. A majority is not necessary. However, if it is the minority who will lead the charge, they need to be strong enough to handle some rocky roads ahead.

Not every church is a candidate for being "replanted". They're not that far gone! Many churches are simply in need of a "transition" or perhaps a "revitalization" instead. While there are differences between the two, certainly a major aspect of replanting is transitioning. You can transition an existing church that is maybe not hitting on all its cylinders, but does need rejuvenation. Perhaps it has simply plateaued - a stage every church experiences. So, unless fresh vision is cast and re-cast, it will never advance. That church may only be taking a nap, needing just a nudge to move forward.

To learn more about the process of leading a church to adopting and fulfilling a fresh, new vision, the book Transitioning by my friend, Dan Sutherland, is most helpful. Flamingo Road Baptist Church was alive but was spinning its wheels in the south Florida sand. Dan shares the steps to their transition, using the Bible story of Nehemiah. About nine years into our replant, I discovered Dan's book and attended his conference. It was full of what we needed to continue the process.

Replanting is not for napping churches, but for those on life support. Where a transition may be an awakening from a prolonged nap, replanting is CPR.

Somebody grab the defibrillator!

Chapter 2
MOSTLY DEAD IS STILL ALIVE

Whoo-hoo-hoo, look who knows so much. It just so happens that your friend here is only MOSTLY dead. There's a big difference between mostly dead and all dead. Mostly dead is slightly alive. - Miracle Max

When my kids were young, we came upon the movie, "The Princess Bride". I'm not sure if it was marketed for kids or not, but I love it! The quote above comes after Miracle Max is told by Inigo Montoya that the hero, young Westley, is dead.

I cannot think of an example in Scripture of a "dead" church, but I can think of a "mostly dead" one. The Laodicean Church of Revelation 3 is described by Jesus as needing repentance for their disconnect with Him. No doubt they began like all first century churches, a plant not genealogically far from the Apostles and the church of Jerusalem where it all started. New life began with genuine conversions and an excitement to belong to this new community of faith.

But, somehow over time, they became more enamored with material things than with their purpose as a church. Jesus warned them He would "vomit" (my preferred translation) them out of His mouth if there was no drastic turnabout. But He also held out hope they could be rejuvenated. Using one of the great illustrations of the Bible, He said He was standing outside the door of their church, knocking. All that was needed was for someone – anyone in that church – to open the door to Him. And if that happened, His promise was to come in and once again be central to their fellowship, giving them life.

I guess Jesus was saying there was still the chance of life in them.

Churches can become "mostly dead" for any number of reasons. Some, even entire denominations, have turned their back on Scripture and have settled on man-made "traditions" like the Pharisees of Jesus' day. Liberal, mainline denominations which over the 19th and 20th centuries abandoned a high view of Scripture have been in decline for generations.

Others still hold to orthodox beliefs, yet they have lost their passion for reaching the world with the Gospel. Somewhere, vision turned inward. Many mostly dead churches don't know it. The preacher may faithfully proclaim the Gospel each and every Sunday. But if the congregation no longer sees themselves as a community of missionaries, the Gospel is only being preached to the converted.

They might even have seen some growth, but it is strictly membership transfers. The tragedy is their commitment to the right doctrines has blinded them to their pending death as a body. Such was the Ephesian church of Revelation 2. Jesus told them they had *lost their first love* and warned them if they did not change and go back to what made them strong at first, He would remove His presence from them.

As Paul Simon once sang, our church had been "slip sliding away" for thirty years. The decline wasn't swift and sudden, but decades long, so gradual that no one caught on. In its first decade of existence as a new church plant, there had been a harvest of redemption in this little community. Changed lives charge up the saints! An energetic young and multi-talented planter preached hard and won souls. Money was raised. Property purchased, and largely with their own hands, a building constructed. There was a new church in town, the only one of its denomination. I've seen a picture of a Vacation Bible School in the 1950s with 100 children. That had to have been most of the kids in this tiny town!

But suddenly, due to an attempt at church discipline that went south, the demoralized founding pastor resigned. A string of pastors followed, and the church became known for its fights against one another more than for its fight to win souls. In the early 70's, a division over adopting bylaws led to the birth of a "new plant" a few miles up the road. In the 80's, the pastor resigned, only to return a few months later, leading to another defection. By the turn of the next decade, it was a skeleton of its old self, barely hanging on. With the summer months came the influx of vacationers filling up its one hundred seats. But the remainder of the year, from September through May, the local congregation dwindled.

They had lost their purpose as a local church in the community and viewed themselves primarily as a place for the tourists to attend church in the summer. Meanwhile, the local population was exploding with new growth while they shrank.

As do most churches of our tradition, every fall of the year brought a week of "revival". I found it interesting that their bylaws *required* a "revival" every fall and spring. Fiery sermons from guest preachers stirred hearts. Occasionally, someone walked the aisle and was saved. Backsliders came forward to "rededicate" their lives to the Lord.

Quite honestly, those meetings I attended in those four years before accepting the call to pastor the church did have good preaching. But, as is in the case of so many churches that hope for "revival" during a protracted meeting, if there is no discipleship ongoing after the sermons, or if the church never rediscovers her purpose and pursues it with passion, the fire quickly cools and is quenched. Everything just settles back into the old routine. The new converts don't grow, and the backsliders fall back again. It's a cycle that provides false hope at best. "Mostly dead" continues.

But, as Miracle Max said, "Mostly dead is slightly alive". And where there's life, there's hope.

In the year or so before the church called me, some flickers of life began to show like the lingering buds on a dying dogwood in spring. A few years earlier, a retired military couple had moved into the area and settled on Nags Head as their church. In her church background, Marilyn had been taught to witness. She had also been part of a church with a great outreach to children in the community. Her heart was stirred for the kids she passed on the road home every day after work.

So, she and Al began inviting those kids to come to Sunday school, where she took up teaching the elementary-aged children. Using their VW van, they would load up as many kids as would come, love them and teach them about Jesus. Before long, they were driving their van and their station wagon to transport them. This was a sign of life!

Tom, a young father in his twenties, was challenged in one of those fall revival meetings to get serious in his relationship with the Lord. Up to that point, church and his personal walk with Christ were not that high on his list of priorities. A good father and husband, he was working his hardest to provide for his wife and three young daughters. God's Spirit was kindling a fire in his heart. This was another sign of life!

Both Tom and his wife Sandra, along with Marilyn and Al, began praying for their church. Others, I'm sure, were doing the same. They realized if there wasn't a renewal that lasted more than a few days, their church had no future. A holy discontent had settled within them. Mostly dead became ominous. But, sparks were beginning to fly. Good sparks.

I learned as a Boy Scout building campfires that often a smoldering fire only needs a blast of fresh air to ignite into a blaze. As a church planter makes it priority to evangelize, a church replanter must make it a priority to fan what coals remain. By that I mean he must find those sparks of life – those parishioners within whom God is at work- and fan the flame. How is that done?

First, you have to **identify the live embers**. I'm not talking about questioning someone's salvation. Rather, find out who has that holy discontent. You listen and observe. When Christians have a real passion for seeing God move, you'll see and hear it. It's not private. Their actions and their words will reveal their hearts. Watch their lives. If there's a spark, their actions will prove their words to be true.

How easy is it to say (or even pray), "I love the Lord and want to see Him bless my church", but then act in ways that quench God's Spirit? Talk is cheap. Look for the passion in their service. And that can't be done at a distance. That requires a keen eye and some ability to discern. Believe it or not, some church folks will say what they think the pastor wants to hear!

A second step is to simply **spend time with the church**. You must devote time with people in the church, getting to know them. It wasn't long before I grabbed young Tom and began investing in his life. God was at work in him before I arrived, and I was going to join in. If he was a diamond in the rough, I wanted to be a tool in the Polisher's hand.

Attend group or committee meetings, if you have such a thing. On second thought, I'll venture that the majority of "mostly dead" churches are on committee overload. Ironically, ours really had no committees. The whole church was a committee!

Invite segments of the church over to your home or to meet at the church for dessert, coffee, conversation and prayer. You can learn a lot about someone by hearing him/her pray. It's like listening to a spiritual stomach growl. There's a hunger for God. And here's a hint: it doesn't focus on Sister Sally's gout attack. It hungers for renewal and for souls.

There's no need to attempt a replant in a dead church. I've learned that when first responders find a body is cold or stiff, CPR is a waste of energy. Dead means totally lifeless. But, in reality, **few churches that were once truly alive are truly dead**. The heartbeat may be faint, the breathing shallow. It will take a miracle, not from Max but from God, but if you'll find the life points, you have somewhere to begin.

One recent summer, our nephew lived with us and enjoyed getting on our riding mower and cutting our grass. I was glad to let him do it. But the first time around the front yard, he accidentally drove our riding mower over two young shrubs in our yard, cutting them down to the nub. I'm no horticulturist, but my hope was that as long as the roots were still able to receive nourishment, the shrubs could make a comeback. My wife was not so hopeful. "They're dead."

Guess what? A year later (no nephew on the mower), I was careful to drive around them. It's yet to be seen how healthy they'll become, but both have grown at least twelve inches high.

"Mostly dead is still alive." There's the hope to start!

Chapter 3
BABY STEPS

In 1991, our church had a used photocopier purchased a couple years earlier from a bank for peanuts. It was a step forward when the church voted to spend a few hundred dollars for it, seeing as how they had never owned a copier before. Problem was, it had not been used for at least six months when I arrived because it had "broken down" ...whatever that meant. No one really knew what was wrong or what it might cost to repair it.

So, there it sat, unused. Rather than see about getting it fixed, it just sat there collecting dust. Like any form of modern technology, once you start using it and begin to discover the advantages it provides, it is hard to go backward and try to survive without it. That is, unless you really never did much with it to begin with.

The idea came up to me from a new attender about the church producing a bulletin each Sunday. You know, with announcements, prayer requests, order of service. Other churches printed off bulletins each Sunday...why not us? Believe it or not, that was something novel to this church. So, I asked some old-timers about it. "What do you think?" "We've never had a bulletin before. Is that necessary?"

Necessary? No. Helpful? Sure.

To produce the bulletin (after the typing, and that's another story), we would either have to find a commercial printer to give us the fifty to seventy-five copies needed, or we could use the copier after getting it fixed and dusted off. "But we were told it would cost more to fix it than it's worth." Really? How do you know that? "Someone somebody knows told us it wasn't worth the fix".

Guess what I did? You got it. I looked up a copier repair service in the yellow pages (that's how long ago this was) and had them come out to tell us what we had to do to get it running. By the next Sunday, we were in business...with the printer, that is. Even the skeptics were delighted when those first bulletins were placed in their hands on Sunday morning.

A "victory" for change, ever so small, was won.

Change is slow. Maybe I should say **change that lasts comes slowly**. And one reason it should be slow is that it starts with little things.

The #1 all-time most serious mistake incoming pastors make is attempting to change too much, too soon. It seems I've heard, and read, that statement before many times from many sources – usually from tenured saints who've taken ownership of their church. If I've heard it, chances are so has everyone else who seeks to pastor a church. You know (maybe have experienced) the horror stories of the sudden announcement, "We're going to a contemporary music style next Sunday!", or "Instead of passing the offering plate, we're putting a box for your offerings in the foyer".

Bringing change to a church is like watching an episode of "Ice Road Truckers". The load must be delivered. The dangers are around every bend. The road is slippery, and as you travel, you hear the cracking of the ice beneath your wheels. And there's always drama of some kind.

Pastors tend to be an impatient breed, and as someone who's been there, done that, I can add that the younger the pastor, generally the more impatient. How many of us, still wet behind the ears - my "old" veteran pastor boss called his young staff "greenhorns" - fresh out of college (yikes!) or seminary, were full of energy, ideas and vision? We were all "that guy"! And, how many rookie pastors survive longer than a couple of years in an established church? I'm reminded of the saying, "Start fast – don't last".

That impatience must be a major source of frustration among entrenched church members, many of whom have no idea anything at the church needs changing. "What's wrong with our church?" Then, along comes the newly elected or appointed leader – however the church or denomination does such things – who, upon first inspection, sees the cracks and voids that the eyes familiar with the church have missed for years. Called by God to lead and take the Promised Land, some pastors will immediately pull out the sword (or, as I was accused, the machete) and start cutting away.

That reminds me of a scene from the book of Joshua, the story of God replanting the nation of Israel. Before the famine had taken Israel's sons and families across

22

the Sinai to brother Joseph's care in Egypt and the 400 years away from home, God brought them (often kicking and screaming) back to the land He had given them through Father Abraham.

Joshua already had some intelligence on Jericho from the spies he had sent earlier. So, he's got a pretty good idea that taking this fortified, walled city will be a huge undertaking.

It would have been so much easier to settle in Canaan had no one moved in when they left for Egypt. But, easy isn't usually a part of God's plan for us. And **if something is easily gained, it tends to also be easily surrendered**. Just down the road from their successful crossing of the River Jordan awaited the first big change. "Joshua", God said, "Take out Jericho. You can't conquer the land and restore the nation to its land unless Jericho's walls come tumbling down." Something like that. So, as any good leader does, Joshua sets out to do some recon on his own so he can come up with a strategy for this conquest. What he was about to learn was that since this was the Lord's idea to conquer the land, it was also the Lord who would lead the transition.

When Joshua was near Jericho, he looked up and saw a man standing in front of him with a drawn sword in His hand. Joshua approached Him and asked, "Are You for us or for our enemies?"

"Neither," He replied. "I have now come as commander of the LORD's army."

Then Joshua bowed with his face to the ground in worship and asked Him, "What does my Lord want to say to His servant?"

The commander of the LORD's army said to Joshua, "Remove the sandals from your feet, for the place where you are standing is holy." And Joshua did so. – Joshua 5:13-15

The "LORD's army" wasn't the Israelis. It was a common Old Testament description of the heavenly contingent of angels who serve Yahweh. The old King James called them the "heavenly host" or the "host of the Lord". Joshua might have cut his eyes left and right, and seeing no "army" wondered, "Really?"

I find it interesting that the "commander" did not say he was on Joshua's side.

Many Bible scholars smarter than me believe him to be a Christophany – a pre-incarnate appearance of Christ. We all know that *if God is for us, who can be against us?*[5]*,* must have applied here. But, the commander seems to be saying, "I didn't come to choose sides". This wasn't about Joshua, or even Israel or Jericho. This was about the LORD and His eternal plan. The commander of the LORD's army had come to take over.

Jericho was the first step in a plan to conquer the land. It was a plan that would take some time before the land was cleared and it was again the Holy Land. While Jericho, the first item needing changing, fell in just days, the conquest of the land would take them seven years. After forty years of wandering and preparation, they had to go another seven before the change was complete.

This was no overnight success. In many ways, the taking of Jericho would be simple in comparison to what lay ahead. But, God lets us start with the simple and then allows us to grow with each subsequent challenge if we'll patiently learn. And not only will those of us who are leaders learn, those who may at first be reluctant to follow will, with each new step, learn to trust our leadership.

But, it's got to be a God-thing where He takes over.

---

[5] Romans 8:31b

Chapter 4
WEED AND FEED

I love a green lawn. In fact, I plant winter rye over my lawn in October, so it is green until the new grass starts perking up in the Spring. But I also know that not everything in my yard that is green is necessarily grass. So, a couple times a year, I'll put down something called "weed and feed". It fertilizes the good stuff and kills the weeds that would overtake the grass.

As you introduce new things into the life of the church, it won't take long to realize some have become content and comfortable with the status quo. As soon as they begin to realize things are changing, they'll become malcontent and uncomfortable. One of two things will happen.

First, those who had any form of power or influence before the changes will choose to either work against them (and retain power), give up and leave the church altogether, or surrender to the new wave of change and revival.

One of the toughest pills for a replanting pastor to swallow is that some need to leave. Every pastor called by God is a shepherd at heart. We don't want to lose a single sheep, even one who disagrees with us. Surely, we convince ourselves, they'll come around. We pray for them. We walk on eggshells around them. We lose sleep over them and get that queasy feeling in our stomachs with each phone call, text, email or Facebook post from them.

But, let's be real. **If God has called you to replant, He has called you to be His agent for change in leading the church back to life.** Those who will work against you and that change must be converted to the vision, or they must go elsewhere. And that's OK. In fact, it's necessary. A replanter is like a planter in this regard: God gave the vision to you. Your job is to help others see it and embrace it as well. Hopefully, many will. But, some will not.

Those who will not see and embrace the vision must leave for the church to move forward. Covertly or overtly, they will be like a ball and chain, working against your leadership and finding others to join them. Get used to it. Not every church member is a godly, Spirit-filled saint. Read 1 Corinthians 3! That holds true especially when the new pastor comes in with fresh vision. Those who hold positions of power, whether real or perceived, will feel threatened.

One aspect of our church that needed prompt change was our music...or what was being passed as music. Small churches will often allow any willing (or, too often, unwilling) member, or even non-member, to be given leadership positions for which they are woefully unqualified, with the excuse "something is better than nothing". Well, sometimes it might be. In our case, it was not.

Our song leader could sing loud! But, that was pretty much his only qualification. And loud does not mean good. His repertoire was about a dozen hymns. So, in a four-Sunday month, each song was sung at least once. I thought, "We've got these hymnals with hundreds of great hymns and Gospel songs. Let's use them." But, it wasn't going to happen under his leadership.

The same man was also "teaching" the adult Sunday School class. "Teaching" is in quotation marks purposefully. It only took me a few Sundays - really, just one - to know that a change was needed there as well. Fortunately, there were better qualified people whom God had brought on board to take the song leader and teacher jobs. To ease the pain of being removed from two very visible roles, I offered him something new. Normally, that's a good move.

I probably should interject here that this brother had been ordained somewhere in his past in a church in another state. While he had never served as a pastor, he fancied himself as one. Later, I was told he would commonly introduce himself as the "associate pastor" of the church. Problem was, he was not. Never had been.

And one more detail. He had lobbied to be the new pastor of the church. The previous pastor knew what a disaster that would be, and the people, even though they endured his song leadership and teaching, weren't about to let that happen. So, he wasn't exactly thrilled when they called me. My arrival spelled the end of his dream.

In the few weeks since we arrived, we were seeing more and more children coming to church, whether being given a ride by a couple in their VW van or with their parents.

A new family in town found us and began attending with their five children! Suddenly, a little church that a few months earlier had two young children, now had nearly twenty coming every Sunday.

Part of my vision was to establish a children's worship service as soon as practical. I'm a believer in kids being taught at their own level. We also believe that there can be no ministry without a minister. So, I thought this displaced brother with a heart to pastor could lead children's worship every Sunday. His wife could help him. He actually jumped at the idea.

That seemed to work well for a while. He was finding fulfillment in teaching the kids. His wife loved being with children. We found some curriculum that would work and turned him loose.

Oops. Have I mentioned that you'll make mistakes along the way?

One Sunday afternoon, the dad of the family with five kids pulled into my driveway. As I greeted him at the door, I could tell he wasn't a happy camper. In his hands were several copies of little booklets that preached the Gospel and, also, dealt with other topics that would have been relevant to teenagers or college students. They were not geared toward grade school kids. One of the booklets dealt with STDs. Without my knowledge (and at that time in our little church, all the ministry leaders came under my leadership), our new children's minister was distributing these to elementary school aged kids on Sundays. He thought he was doing a good thing.

"Look what he gave my kids at church on Sunday!" I wanted to find a hole to crawl in. This was totally unacceptable. This was on my watch. I had given this man the ministry position, and I'm a believer in "the buck stops here". **Leadership is not only the top rung on the ladder, it's also the most precarious.**

I only had one choice. That week, before the next Sunday, I had relieved him of his kids' ministry. He had blown whatever trust he needed from parents. Fortunately (again), God was involved and already had a very capable and experienced, spiritually mature woman ready in the wings. By the way, she was also new to the church but had been in my Tuesday night Bible study, so I knew her well.

Our brother, who now had been removed from three ministry positions in a short period of time, would soon move on. To his credit, I don't remember him trying to stir up any trouble, as will often happen. He and his wife quietly slipped away to another church where he found opportunities to serve. But, he just couldn't fit in with the vision we were building upon.

I'm a firm believer in the church being the body of Christ, and that **the Holy Spirit places those in the body who will be productive and cooperative within the body.** See 1 Corinthians 12:1-11. And since the Spirit has that role, He also has the role of moving people out who no longer work with what He is trying to accomplish. **The role of the pastor/replanter is to be in tune with the Spirit and follow His lead.**

Years later, I heard Rick Warren say that when there are people who don't agree with the vision or just can't, or won't, fit in for whatever reason, you have to let them go. But, you get to choose who leaves. As a leader, you must establish standards and expectations in advance, so the contrary and the square pegs can move on.

And if they move on, don't be surprised that God has someone ready to fill in the gaps - someone who will get it and get it right.

When you accept that some will leave and some will need to leave, then, as a pastor, you can get focused on doing the things that will bring growth and health to the church. First and foremost, that would be your ability to get into the Word and get them into it as well. If you're not putting out fires you didn't start, you can zero in on preparing the sheep for God's fire to burn within them to reach their community.

Chapter 5

EITHER FISH OR CUT BAIT

Like most churches of our denomination, our "membership" roll was padded with names of people who had joined the church in years gone by and now were nowhere to be found on Sundays (or any other time, for that matter). In fact, some were unknown to the current "active" members. Sound familiar?

People, with mostly good intentions, join the church through whatever process the church observes. In our tradition, that involves coming forward during an altar call, shaking the pastor's hand and having the church vote on the spot to receive. In all my years in Baptist churches, I've never heard/seen a "no" vote. Most of them begin to attend regularly. Some even commit themselves to being contributors, not just consumers. But gradually over time, a percentage of those members become MIA – missing in action - for any number of reasons. As easy as it was to join, it is just as easy to vanish. Easy come, easy go.

Some move away and either never find another church to join, or if they do, the new church home doesn't notify the former church of the move. That's not untypical when the move is to a fellowship of another flavor. Early on, their friends may know where they are, but, after a few years of zero contact due to distance, they become just names and numbers to help you with your stats.

Some just drop out for reasons never expressed (or never sought).

☐ *Personal crisis.* One couple in our church abruptly stopped attending. Weeks later, I caught up with them and asked, "Where have you been?" It turned out they were in a financial bind, and their car insurance had lapsed, so they weren't driving. Trying not to let them see my eyes rolling, I said, "You should have said something. We could have helped." But, some people really don't get the community and caring aspects of a church. They only see an institution.

☐ *Ruffled feathers.* Something was said, done or *perceived* that caused offense. And rather than take a biblical approach as outlined by Jesus in Matthew 18 for handling wrongs, they chose to be non-confrontational, angry and absent. Perception, by the way, is reality for too many in the church who never seek to resolve differences or misunderstandings. The easy route is to drop out or go somewhere else rather than find grace and resolution.

☐ *Preferences.* We all know how "worship wars", for example, have caused an explosion in church "plants" and in transfer membership. If you change *anything,* it seems someone's going to get a burr in his saddle. There are some things, such as doctrine, that should never change. But, Christians seem to have a tough time separating convictions from preferences.

☐ *Unrealized expectations.* You'll see this the first time the pastor doesn't visit someone in the hospital. "We left the church because obviously the pastor doesn't love us". Or even better, "The pastor only has time for a few special friends and we're not in that group apparently. So, we left to find a church where we're appreciated." I've had people have surgery, and I never knew about it. I guess they figure God should have told me, because they never did. They get hurt, and they vanish.

☐ *Greener pastures*. Everyone loves new things. At first, the new church relationship is exciting and full of discoveries. And while that's all great, it's a shallow excuse for personal spiritual growth that produces a "new" relationship with the mercies of God every day. And if that relationship isn't being fostered, the need for something new focuses on programs and sermons. Like a new car, the smell eventually fades. When that happens. they get antsy and start looking elsewhere for that "newness". It's a repetitive cycle, by the way.

☐ *"I wasn't being fed".* That line is every pastor's favorite. Guess what? If you've been a believer for more than a year, it's time to pick up your own fork and knife and begin feeding yourself. But, word gets out that the new pastor at the church up the road is a *real* teacher. So, off they go. 1 Corinthians 3 and Hebrews 5 talk about those who continue to exist on milk as spiritually mature infants, rather than meat and at the place where they can begin to teach others. "I wasn't being fed" is most often a sign of immature selfishness.

Don't misunderstand. We still have people occasionally fall through the cracks or walk away for these very reasons (and probably a few I haven't thought of).

Frequently in our elders' meetings, we'll ask, "Have you seen so-and-so lately?". And the larger the congregation, the more likely you'll have vanishing members. But the issue here is, do you continue to call them "members"?

And so, most churches have as many as two or three times their average Sunday attendance still listed as "members". It looks good on their annual reporting to the denomination. In our denomination, a church's number of "messengers" (delegates) to denominational meetings is determined by membership. So, why take people off the roll? You only lose your voice at the convention. Right?

The dirty little secret is that the inflated number of members give pastors a reason to puff our chests out a bit more at pastors' fellowships and, maybe more importantly, on our resumes. So, to claim a realistic membership based on committed and active participants would pop that balloon in a hurry.

But what is the "church"? If it boils down to a dusty list kept in a book or on a digital spreadsheet by the church clerk, does it at all resemble what Christ intended? If it includes people who have not given, not served, not prayed with nor even attended in years (sometimes even decades), how can it be called a "body"? I mean, if I woke up tomorrow and my right hand was suddenly missing, I'd want to know where it went. If my left eye wasn't working, how long would it be before I visited the ophthalmologist?

Paul seemed to be clear in his letters to the churches that not only should every believer belong to a local church, but that everyone who belongs does so to contribute in an active way.

> From Him the *whole* body, fitted and knit together by *every supporting ligament*, promotes the growth of the body for building up itself in love by the proper working of *each individual part*. - Ephesians 4:16 (Emphasis mine).

To the struggling Corinthian church, he wrote:

> A manifestation of the Spirit is given to *each person to produce* what is beneficial... - 1 Corinthians 12:7 (My emphasis again).

The historian Luke recorded that those 3,000 on the Day of Pentecost who believed and were baptized became part of the Jerusalem church.

So those who accepted his message were baptized, and that day about 3,000 people were *added to them*. – Acts 2:41 (Yes, I'm still emphasizing).

Also, check Paul's words to the Roman church in Romans 12:3-10 about using the gifts God gives to *benefit* the church. **An uninvolved "member" really isn't a member.**

With that being said, the idea of an "inactive member" is really a contradiction of terms. So, let's stop pretending about who is part of our churches.

In January of 1991, Nags Head Baptist Church had a grand total of sixty-eight "members". OK. So, that's not very "grand". Yet, in reality, there were about twenty-five who were regular attenders, and even less who participated in ministry, but then that's the case everywhere, isn't it? We were typical of the 20/80 rule where 20% do 80% of the ministry.

Taking a look at the clerk's membership roll, I wondered (aloud to several folks), "Who are these people?" Then, I began to hear about some of them who had moved to another state or were unknown. We even found that more than one was in eternity. I was told that a few years earlier the church had sent out letters to absentee members, urging them to return, with the goal of cleaning up the roll. Even then, however, no one had been removed for fear of hurting someone's feelings.

There's no sense starting off a replant with imaginary people. Church plants don't have that luxury! It didn't take me long to send out another letter and make some phone calls and personal visits to those I could find, inviting them to return "home". These forty some "members", however, had been gone too long, and had either connected with other churches or had no desire to return, many for the reasons cited earlier.

As I recall, our total membership "grew" quickly from 68 to 43. The number went down but it was truly positive growth. In those first few months, we had received a number of new members. Forty-three isn't a big church by any stretch. But when all of them are active and discovering what it means to do and be a church, things have a way of progressing.

I know that some, whom I greatly respect, tell us to never remove "inactive" members, hoping that an open door will bring them back. **If your concept of membership doesn't require some sense of commitment and active participation, why have it?** And if you're the pastor, an elder or one of the deacons, you are accountable to the Chief Shepherd for those unknown sheep. How can you shepherd sheep who either have long ago left the flock or, maybe also, no longer want to be part of it? I don't believe you can or that you should.

Of course, you go after a wandering sheep. Certainly, an effort must be made to reclaim lost sheep. Jesus said that's what shepherds do. But if after honest, sincere efforts you discover they have no desire to come back, you have to let them go. You'll have enough to do with the sheep who are in the fold. Put your focus on them.

Chapter 6

FOCUSED DISCIPLESHIP -INVESTING IN POTENTIAL LEADERS

One of the challenges most pastors face is their calling to give spiritual leadership to an entire congregation while being a disciple-maker at the same time. The dilemma is that no one person can truly help more than a few believers – especially those who have years of nominal spiritual growth behind them – become radical learners and followers of Christ. Disciple-making pastors have learned they alone cannot accomplish the Great Commission. But they must do their parts, and that begins with focusing on a few and investing in them.

Early in my ministry, I learned Paul's strategy for raising up disciples. He shared it with his own protégé, Timothy, when he wrote to him, *And what you have heard from me in the presence of many witnesses, commit to faithful men who will be able to teach others also.*[6] While Timothy was in Ephesus providing leadership to a struggling church – one that Paul had established and was heavily invested in –, he was to find men…"faithful" is the key word…to teach who would continue the cycle after he was gone.

Of course, **in a replant, finding truly "faithful" men might be a challenge.** It's common to find that many, if not most, are long-term spiritual babes.[7] Nothing in their experience has aroused a hunger for growth in years. So, they've settled for the status quo, even in their own discipleship.

But even in the church of Laodicea in Revelation 3, the implication was that someone was in the church holding on to the faith. It was to that person Jesus made the invitation to "open the door", so He could spend quality time with him. **And that's what discipleship is about more than anything: spending quality time with the learner.** Most important in a replant is finding that person(s) who has leadership potential.

Making that discovery may take some time. Mostly, it takes observation and

---

[6] 2 Timothy 2:2
[7] 1 Corinthians 3:1-3

rubbing shoulders. A great tool for both is for the pastor to call for (and likely organize at this stage) some "work days" at the church campus. Whether it's painting or pulling weeds, great relationships can be built on Saturday mornings sprucing up the building and grounds. And there you find people who at least are committed to the property. And that's a start.

Prayer that asks God to bring the cream to the top is also vital for the pastor. Nothing is more frustrating than investing time and energy in someone who will do nothing with it. That's why Paul stressed "faithful" men. Because He knows the hearts of the members, He also knows the diamonds in the rough. Ask Him to bring that one or two to the forefront.

Jesus' example should make it clear to us that this kind of disciple-building and leader training should not be done with a crowd. Though He had crowds listening to His sermons, the bulk of His time was devoted to a dozen, and the deeper things He only revealed initially to three – Peter, James and John. So, it should be no surprise that the first recognized leaders of the first church were those same three men.

It was obvious that if our church was to grow and live out God's purposes for us, we needed to infuse the leadership with youth. Being a Baptist church with a traditional polity, the leadership structure included the pastor (me) and the two incumbent deacons, both in their late 80's. One of them saw my calling as opportunity to retire from his office, which he did gracefully. The other deacon, a kindly jack-of-all-trades kind of man, willingly stayed on. He and I would meet when needed. I took him out to visit church members with me, which he seemed to enjoy. But, I knew it was going to take someone younger in leadership to help facilitate the turn-around.

The only other man in the church at the time under 45 was Tom. He and his wife Sandra married when they were still in their teens. They had met as middle school students, and Sandra invited Tom to come to church with her. Both became Christians, and ten years and three children later, they were still in the church when I arrived. As Tom tells it, God used a series of revival meetings that fall to awaken him to his need to be a more consistent Christian, both in his family and in his church. Then, just a couple of months later, the church called me to be his pastor – something he and Sandra supported.

So, here was my "faithful" and younger man. Not long before we started a men's morning Bible study at a local restaurant. Tom was there consistently, and his passion to learn and grow was evident. We spent time together informally as well. He and Sandra were the closest in the church to our ages and had kids the same ages as well. All the while, Tom was growing in his spiritual maturity and becoming a student of the Word. He got involved in our new youth ministry, too, going to student conferences and camps, which spurred on his growth.

In the meantime, a couple of older gentlemen who had come into the church shortly after my arrival became deacons. But we still needed new, young blood in that group, and eventually, it became clear to Tom, to me and to the church that he was ready. Today, more than 25 years later, Tom is still leading. After a couple of years of serving as a deacon, Tom became the third member of our team of pastors, leading our ministry teams. He's proven also to be a very able and gifted Bible teacher and has taken on the role of teaching pastor, occupying the Sunday "pulpit" (we really don't have a pulpit anymore) whenever I need a break.

Soon more faithful men in the church rose to the top and took on leadership roles. I've learned that **faithful men will attract faithful men.** There is something within us guys that causes us to be spurred on by example. Paul was Timothy's role model and mentor. Timothy became the same (we assume) to men in the Ephesian Church. And on and on it goes.

This kind of growth and change takes time. It can't be done from within the walls of the pastor's study. It's done with a shovel in your hand, a cup of coffee around a breakfast table with an open Bible or standing on the beach, casting bottom rigs for flounder.

Don't look for a man who talks a good talk. There's much more to finding potential disciples and leaders. One lesson I learned early on is that **faithful men don't talk about their potential, they demonstrate it by action and attitude.** Jesus found fishermen mending their nets, which told Him that even when there were no fish to catch that day, they were not lazy and were getting prepared for the next time out. Character and discipline "spoke" loudly from their actions. Too often pastors, in self-imagined desperation, will grab anyone to put into leadership. That almost never ends up well. The good talkers are usually just that...good at talking. Living it escapes them.

As you replant, you'll need doers. If God has you there to be His vessel through which He breathes new life into the church, He also has someone, or two or three, within whom He has placed a readiness to do whatever they can to help you turn the ship around. Pray for them. Watch for them. Then, invest in them.

Chapter 7

REDISCOVERING THE CHURCH

Valvoline motor oil had a commercial that went something like this: A group of six adults, riding in a car billowing smoke from the exhaust, is in a funeral procession. The man in the back seat asks the driver, "What kind of motor oil do you use?" In a monotone, the driver replies, "Motor oil is motor oil". Of course, the point Valvoline wanted to make was, "No, it isn't".

I'm no car mechanic. Sure, I can pop open the hood and do some minor repairs myself. And, occasionally, I'll change the oil myself. What do I do? I go to Wal-Mart or NAPA and look for the best deal on oil. But, don't think that because I'm not a real mechanic I don't know that some oils are better than others. I've heard the word "viscosity" before. It has something to do with the oil not breaking down...I think. And I know there are letters on the packaging. SAE something or another. And there's numbers, too. 10W this and that.

So, I know that not all motor oils are the same. But I haven't a clue why. Mostly what I know is that if you don't change it every few thousand mile, your engine is in jeopardy of major damage. I do know that much! My 17-year-old Dodge truck is still going with nearly 240,000 miles. I've kept the oil changed.

In some ways, the church is like an automobile engine. Lots of parts. When they all work together, the church purrs like a well-tuned engine. But, when it hasn't been properly maintained, the parts fail...or they give up...or they squeak so loud the rest of the parts get tired and want out.

It's not that they're bad parts necessarily. Ephesians 4:16 tells us that God put the parts in the church as He desired. *From Him the whole body, fitted and knit together by every supporting ligament, promotes the growth of the body for building up itself in love by the proper working of each individual part.*

Often, it's simply that the "parts" don't have a clue what's under the hood of the church and how it works. I'll take a stab here and say that, in many churches, the members are unable to define what a church is or why it has been assembled.

They just know that church is supposed to be…church. Whatever that means.

Jesus put a lot of hope in the future of the church. He said, *I will build My church, and the forces of Hades will not overpower it.*[8] And that was before there was a church. Quite the prediction. Quite the promise.

When you venture beyond the Gospels into the Acts, you find a church discovering daily[9] who they were. They wrote the book on being the church! God saw to it that their story was written and preserved so the generations of churches could learn from them.

Following the Acts are a string of letters, mostly written to local churches or to Paul's protégés serving churches. In those letters, Paul defines the church, corrects church problems, and sets standards for leaders and followers, all the while detailing the relationship between the church and Christ.

Even in the Revelation, before all the visions and beasts and demonic creatures of the Tribulation and beyond, Jesus sends letters to seven churches in Asia Minor that reveal His heart for who they should be.

My point? **There seems to be plenty – more than enough – doctrine of the church in the New Testament for us to know who we are.** But can the average Joe (or Josephine) in the pew give an accurate definition of the church? Is the purpose and mission of the church clearly understood by most church members? If one hundred parishioners in the same church were asked, "Why does the church exist?", would there be one hundred different answers? Worse, would there be silence?

Could it be that one reason dying churches are gasping for air is because they really don't know who they are? Somewhere in their past, ecclesiology has become a forgotten subject. Tradition – you know, that plague that eventually sucks the life out of the church, that causes us to never compare our practices with Scripture and assumes that the way we've been doing it must be right – replaces a passion to do God's work God's way.

---

[8] Matthew 16:18
[9] Acts 2:46-47

If the church is one generation from extinction, it doesn't take long – maybe less than a decade – for the faithful to forget. And when there's a revolving door to the pulpit, as there is in many churches, there's no wonder that a consistent grasp of church doctrine is not to be found.

Our church was like so many: good, well-meaning people trying to do what they thought was the right thing. The solid foundation on which to build was in their hands. The knowledge of how to apply it was missing. As a result, they weren't even maintaining. They were losing ground. **One of my first priorities was to teach from Scripture what God had to say about the church.**

We've become so accustomed to calling the building where the body of Christ gathers "the church" that many – maybe most in "the church" - see the church that way. Even if we know that the church is people, not property, we still call the brick and mortar "the church". I confess, I do it. I'll set up a meeting with someone and tell him or her to come to "the church" where I'll be in my office. But do you wonder if the people in the pew have never heard that they are the church? More than that, do they know what that entails?

Like most traditional churches of our denomination, we met Sunday mornings for Sunday school, preaching, Sunday evenings for more preaching, and Wednesday nights for prayer. That weekly calendar, which worked well when it was established generations ago, needed a fresh look. You've heard it before... those who come on Sunday morning love the church, those who come on Sunday night love the pastor and those who come on Wednesday night love the Lord.

Sunday nights were attended by those with a stronger commitment to the church and the Word. At least, that's how it seemed. But, as one old deacon said to me, "We've got nothing else to do!", so they came to church. How's that for a motive?

I really didn't fit their image of a "preacher", even on Sunday mornings. ("You do more 'teaching' than you do 'preaching'"). But on Sunday nights, the "teacher" in me came out even stronger. So, the very first series I taught was on the doctrine of the church. I titled it "God's Work God's Way". And for several weeks – maybe ten or twelve – we used Ephesians 4:11-16 as our foundational text on who we were as a church and who God wanted us to be. Starting off with ecclesiology gave me the chance to lay the foundation of purpose that would take us through every transition ahead. **If you don't know who you are, how can you expect to understand what it is you are to do?**

In that Ephesians passage, Paul says volumes about the church. To the credit of the previous pastors, ours was a church that historically recognized the authority of Scripture to speak into their lives. As I opened this passage in a word by word fashion, they listened and seemed to agree. New concepts were introduced. Of course, they weren't really "new" - they were 2,000 years old. But, for most of these believers, it was new to them due to generations of traditions. There's a marvelous dynamic that happens when we uncover buried treasure in God's Word. We get hungry to dig and know more.

I taught them about the role of the pastor-teacher (that was a new term for them) in equipping them to be "ministers". Ministers? That really played with their minds because for most Christians, just as the church is a building, the "minister" is the ordained cleric. And here I was telling them we were all "ministers", that God had given each of them a gift for

serving the church, and when we all did our part, the church would be healthy and grow.

Clear teaching on the church didn't just reveal "new" concepts for revitalizing the church, it also served to dispel any misconceptions that seem to breed in churches where teaching doctrine is sacrificed on the altar of "evangelism". The start to church health is finding balance between evangelism and edification. It can't be "either/or". It must be both. Sadly, although our church's preaching history was one of Gospel and holiness (with a bit of a legalistic flavor), conversions and baptisms were rare. But they believed they were doing the best they could.

Belief leads to behavior. In replanting, the behavior is in obvious need of an upgrade. But for that to happen, you may need to dust off the belief first. Help them get a handle on "the church". Teach ecclesiology.

An interesting side note that exemplifies a lack of knowledge of the doctrine of the church: As I was writing this chapter, I was also involved in a conversation on Facebook about pastors. One lady in on the chat said, "Not all pastors lead a church...but they can have tremendous impact on individuals". She then proceeded to quote from Acts 20:28 and Ephesians 4:11-12 as proof texts, totally disregarding the fact that both passages were written to real local churches, not some mystical "church" that's "out there".

Ecclesiology, like any doctrine, needs to be "sound"[10], which requires a consistent hermeneutic. This lady's understanding of the office or role of pastor was based on an ecclesiology that, like a jigsaw puzzle missing a piece or two, was incomplete. Only churches have pastors, and without a church to lead, there is no pastor.

To be an effective pastor requires gaining a measure of their trust. That's next.

---

[10] Titus 2:1

Chapter 8

EARNING TRUST – LEARNING TO TAKE IT SLOW!

Q: How many (*fill in your denominational brand here*) does it take to change a light bulb?

A: CHANGE?!

We chuckle. But the horror stories abound. Every pastor who takes an existing church, that perhaps has been in neutral for a while, has the sense that God has called him to be the catalyst for change. That's especially true of the younger pastors – the fresh-out-of-seminary guys. Like young racehorses corralled for three years, they're ready to bolt from the starting gate and lead by speed. Holding them back takes every bit of the jockey's skill and strength.

Like so many seminary students with a young family, I was financially at the bottom rung of the ladder. So, saving money was a necessity. When my car was clearly in need of a tune up, I decided to change the spark plugs myself, even though my spark plug experience was limited to the lawn mower. So, off to Kmart I went.

With the right plugs in hand, I began to gap (someone told me how to do that) and replace the plugs. I was careful to do them one at a time, so that I put the correct wire back on each new plug. With 6 cylinders, the job didn't take long, and when it was done, I stood back and admired my work! But, when I started it up and took her for a test drive, it ran rough as a cob. Up went the hood. Again, each new plug was removed and put back in to make sure they were properly seated and that each wire was truly connected. They were.

But, it still ran rough.

I had heard the expression "running on all eight" before and vaguely understood its meaning. Now I had first-hand experience with an engine that wasn't hitting

45

on all six cylinders. With no other option, I took it to a mechanic. Not only did he quickly diagnose the problem, but that day it was back in my hands running like...like a well-tuned engine. It seems that my lack of experience caused me to over-tighten one of the plugs, putting a hairline crack in its porcelain and rendering the plug defective. Who knew? Not me!

Even though I had removed that plug and put it back in, it never crossed my mind to carefully examine it for a crack. But that was the culprit. A new plug was the simple remedy.

The church that is running on all eight cylinders after a pastoral resignation, retirement or death is both blessed and rare. However, if the previous pastor's exit was a "forced termination", you can bet that there is disease present. Something that may, or may not, be easy to be detected is cracked. It may not be terminal yet, but the symptoms are undeniable, at least to an objective eye. And if it is only running on six or seven cylinders, someone has to lift the hood and find out why. A good pastor is a trained church mechanic and knows how to spot the fouled plug or clogged injector.

In a car, you simply replace, tweak or flush out the problem. In a church, you can do that, but chances are it will stir up a mess from those who have accepted a less than smooth running engine. After all, if their only church experience is in a less-than-healthy church, they probably think it is normal. And just because you're the new marshal in town doesn't mean everyone is going to accept your badge. Not at first. But, trust can be earned if you take the time.

The problem too often is us. We pastors, especially the younger among us, are not necessarily the patient type. And because (most of us) are men, we're by nature "fixers". "If it needs fixin', I'll fix it and fix it now". So, we pull out our electric drill, put on the Phillips head driver and torque it down. Zap! Done!

But not everyone in the congregation was willing to accept that a fix was in order. Sometimes, we need to forego the drill and simply use a screw driver, turning the screw slowly. Later, we can come back and turn it one more time. Eventually, you get the same result as the drill, but the fix, because it was over a period of time, is barely noticeable.

A dying church likely needs an overhaul of vision and strategy. So, where to start?

First, **take on the minor things**. Some changes aren't major yet will make a difference.

I related the story in chapter 3 about the copier and the bulletin. That's really a minor change. Installing the phone and answering machine - minor changes. Then, there was the time in my first month, when I told the deacons/ushers that we wouldn't be receiving the offering until the end of the service. And even though one of them looked at me oddly and said, "I never "heerd" of such a thing", they went with it and it was OK. Minor, small changes.

And keep in mind that some changes that seem minor to you, might be major to them. An example might be changing the times of Sunday school and worship. Surely you realize that 11:00 has been the time church has started since apostolic days? That would be, in most churches, a major change.

Second, **give it time**. Let me go back to my earlier illustration from *The Princess Bride*. The hero of the story, Westley, has had his life taken away by the cruel Prince Humperdinck. But his friends find him and bring him to Miracle Max, the local miracle man. As Max examines Westley, his friend Inigo says, "Sir, we're in a terrible rush", to which Max replies, "Don't rush me, sonny. You rush a miracle man, you get rotten miracles."

His prognosis is that Westley is not dead, but "mostly dead", and concocts a pill to bring him back to life, with the instruction that, "you have to wait fifteen minutes before potency" and "he shouldn't go swimming for at least an hour". Don't you love that scene? You don't want rotten miracles!

Changes, no matter how "noble" or necessary, that are impatiently rushed into being will end up as failures. Leaders always struggle with the tension between the urgency of life returning versus the time it takes to build strong foundations and earn the confidence of the church first. And, along with patience, it takes a measure of wisdom from on High to know when to make those first moves.

As "Rome wasn't built in a day", neither can a church be rebuilt in a year, or two or three for that matter. Working against so many churches and pastors is the prevailing wind that says if things don't change quickly, it's time for a new captain at the wheel. And either the pastor gives up too soon, or the church grows weary of so much change so suddenly and removes him. The church then goes back to ground zero, undoing most of what has been done, and the pastor has another couple of lines to add to his resume.

If your church needs a "miracle", don't rush it. You'll be tempted to be in a hurry to get things done. Miracles happen, but always on His timetable, not ours. Reflect on a couple that Jesus performed when He knew the time was right.[11]

The key to enacting patient, effective change isn't about new ideas or demographics or copying this model or that. The key is to **develop relationships** within the church. The Bible is chock full of admonitions regarding relationships. And what is the church if it isn't a community built around them? Here's what happens when the pastor seeking to replant takes time and energy to cultivate friendships within the church.

☐ *Trust is earned.* As the church gets to know you, they learn that either you are worthy of their trust, or you are not. With genuine friendships, we get to know one another. If your motives are clear and it's obvious you are on board to help *them* advance in their journey of being disciples, you'll be earning that trust. But if the church senses in a new pastor that they are simply your stepping stone to something bigger and better, and that you are there more for you than for them, trust will never be gained.

☐ *Strength is acquired.* With change will come opposition. Ask Nehemiah. Every leader will face his detractors. But when the leader is working on building a solid network of friends who trust him and are loyal to him as friends, the leader is no longer standing alone. There is strength in numbers. Solomon (a wise man) noted, *And if somebody overpowers one person, two can resist him. A cord of three strands is not easily broken.*[12]

Pastors who lead change realize they cannot do it alone. Meet folks for lunch or coffee. Visit with them in their homes and invite them to yours. Go hunting/fishing/golfing with them. Just hang out. Start a mens group of some kind. Work with them, getting your hands dirty on church work days. And, by all

---

[11] Mark 5:21-43 and John 11:1-45

[12] Ecclesiastes 4:12

means, don't leave the ladies out. Just be sure you have boundaries in place and include your wife.

☐ *Creativity is encouraged.* Believe it or not, the pastor is not the only person with good ideas! Within every dying church is someone longing for things to change. Find that person and get to know him or her.

☐ *Longevity is probable.* It's hard to leave a church full of friends, especially when you have much invested in them. Lifeway researcher Thom Rainer has found that long-term pastorates are a common denominator in healthy, growing churches.

By the way, this goes against conventional wisdom that has for years told us that we pastors should not build friendships within the churches we pastor. Of course, that line of thinking perpetuates the pastoral revolving door. Church is community, not isolationism.

Earn points. Although it sounds secular and self-serving, it is the biblical concept of gaining favor with those we serve. Proverbs 11:30 (NLT) tells us, *The seeds of good deeds become a tree of life; a wise person wins friends.* As we take on the challenges of the small things that can make a difference, we need to lead without pushing and cultivate relationships. "Victories" in bringing about the necessary changes for the church to return to the life God desires for it will result in us "earning points" or "making deposits" in our community bank. And here's why that is so important.

Not every attempt at correction or change will succeed. In fact, failure is not only inevitable, it is also our best teacher. And with failure will be the need for the church to extend a kind of forgiveness, so that rather than react in anger or confusion, they'll put that failed idea behind them and be willing to go on to what's next.

We've learned over the years to call our new ideas for ministry, strategy and outreach "experiments". Sometimes, what we think we need to do just won't work for any number of reasons. If it is an experiment, it is easier to say, "Wow. That didn't go like we thought. Let's go back to the drawing board."

For us it has been things like Vacation Bible School and Community Pancake

Breakfasts. Now you know. We have neither Sunday School or Vacation Bible School. And we're a Baptist church!

Because our church community is in a very linear geographically, meaning our partners are spread out over as much as 75 miles away, and not in a typical town with a radius of a few miles, VBS just didn't fly. It had been years since the church did VBS. So, in my early years, we tried to establish one. But it just didn't work. So, after about 3 or 4 years of trying (and spending significant dollars) we canned it. Now, we do other summer things for kids.

A few years ago, I heard of a church that hosted a community pancake breakfast on the Sunday following Christmas. The concept was to not have a Sunday worship gathering, but to instead invite our local, unchurched community to drop in between 9 and 11 and get a free breakfast. It was the "if you feed them, they will come" idea. We even ventured out the Sunday night prior with teams of carolers going through local neighborhoods, singing and giving out a nicely done invitation to breakfast "on us". There was no preaching. No overt evangelism. Just a welcome to the community.

Problem was, no one came. OK, maybe a handful showed up. And we tried this two consecutive years and got the same results. It might have worked great in Iowa, but not so much in Nags Head. It was a failed experiment. But, that's OK. We got an A for trying! No one got his shorts in a bunch the next year when we didn't go caroling or serve breakfast the last Sunday of the year.

No one of us is the fourth person of the Trinity. Unlike God, the church's trust in our leadership has to be earned. When over time it is, things start moving forward.

Earning their trust then leads to the next step: Creating a Culture of Change.

Chapter 9
CREATING A CULTURE OF CHANGE

Change is a difficult pill for most of us to swallow. We actually fear change because with it comes the unknown of "we've never done it this way before". The path to the unknown takes trust, which is another word for faith. And what is a church if not a community of faith?

In the previous chapter, I noted that before change happens, trust has to be earned. But in the church, change doesn't stop with the first thing you do differently. I'd say it has a starting point, but after more than a quarter century of changes they're still ongoing. They may not be as rapidly or as big, but for a church to move forward ("move" is an important word), something is always changing.

Already I've talked about the baby steps of change - those little things that make little waves, but don't threaten to overturn the ship because they simply make sense. Things like installing a telephone in the church office.

When I started as the interim part-time pastor, it was necessary for me to have a place - a quiet place - to study. At home were three home-schooled children in elementary school. There was no quiet place in our modest home! But, the church had a room that at one time had been the tiniest of classrooms and now was used for storage. With a little work, it would become my office.

A desk and chair were donated. Bookshelves were installed. Blinds put up on the window. But, in those days before cell phones, there was no telephone in the building. I inquired as to why and was told that a decade or so earlier, a phone line was put in and a phone installed. But with limited finances something had to be dropped, and since the phone was rarely, if ever used, they got rid of it. And, I was told, it never worked right anyway.

So, I lobbied that if I was going to spend hours in the new office, it would be great to have a phone for communication. And, should there ever be an emergency at the church, a phone on the premises would be invaluable for calling 911. All that made sense to them. We purchased a phone, called the phone company, and in days had a connection to the outside world! And it worked!

But I took it up a notch. "Let's also purchase an answering machine". I wasn't always going to be in the office, so anyone who needed to get me or find out about the church could call and leave a message. And when they called, we could record a greeting giving service times. You could see the wheels turning in the business meeting. This was a decision that at the time necessitated a church vote! So, with a little discussion, a "second" was made and the next day I purchased a $35 answering machine.

Soon we were replacing the old dilapidated church sign with a new, modern sign in a new location, not on the side street but on the main highway that ran beside our property. Such a small change was well over-due, and it spoke volumes to our community about what was happening inside the building.

I have no qualms about using a modern English version of the Bible. If we're going to communicate the most precious truths of Scripture, why not use the language of the culture? After about six months, I made the subtle change of teaching from the KJV to the NKJV. In doing so, I let them know that they would note some differences, but the differences would not be so drastic they could not follow in their Bibles. Of course, that change led to many buying their own NKJV. And we soon replaced the pew Bibles with the newer version as well. And let me add, there were no complaints. Why not? As I said, the change was subtle, and they were learning to go with change.

Those little changes early on paved the way for bigger changes down the road. We were intentionally creating a culture of change within a church that had not changed in 40 years. I talked about changes and the theology of change that takes place in us if we are to grow and mature as believers. The gospel is all about change! Those little changes brought little, if no, resistance.

But, there are changes that will cause the swell of resistance to rise!

In less than three years, we assembled a committee of men and women who were mature in their walk with the Lord and drafted a new Constitution and Bylaws. It not only spelled out our beliefs but brought about a major revolution in our church polity. Home meetings were organized to go through it with the members and respond to their questions. When it came time at the church's annual meeting, the overwhelming majority saw it as being both biblical and healthy for the church. We did lose a handful of members over it. Some still acted as though Roberts' Rules had to be somewhere in the Bible, but was found nowhere in the bylaws! It was one of two major steps we took to totally overhaul dead traditions that were stumbling blocks to further growth.

If we were going to reach younger families, our music had to change as well. Probably the biggest visible (and audible) change would be our worship style.

At the start, on Wednesday nights I picked up my guitar and began to teach them "contemporary" worship songs that weren't in the hymnal. Most of those were simple scripture choruses. Before long, perhaps a year later, those songs became a part of a blended Sunday worship experience13. Someone had donated a karaoke machine with a built in cassette player/recorder. We had our first sound system! A couple Radio Shack mics were plugged into it, and we had amplification.

Within a couple of years, a quality sound system was professionally installed. I emphasized that word intentionally. Then an overhead projector (remember them?) was used to put the words of the songs up on a screen. We were on our way.

In less than ten years, the hymnals we purchased in 1991 (the newest version) were donated to a local nursing home. The large, beautiful oak pulpit and the platform chairs (I called them "thrones") were stored away, as were the dozen chairs in the rarely used choir loft. The partition separating the pulpit area from the choir loft was removed opening up the whole stage. The unused organ was donated to a church who had lost theirs to a flood. The piano was sold and replaced with a digital keyboard, and a full band of volunteers (including drums!) replaced me with my acoustic guitar.

In order to accommodate the growing Sunday morning attendance, we had to go from one to two and then to three worship services. So, we moved Sunday school to Sunday night, replacing our Sunday evening service. And after about a year of that, and seeing no growth, we ended Sunday school altogether and replaced it with small groups. Since the very start, we've had a separate children's worship coinciding with the adult worship, so our kids are being taught at their level on Sundays.

There are several key ingredients to bringing about a culture of change.

---

[13] I'm not a personal advocate of "blended" services. You tend to end up dividing the church. But for us, it was a logical transition from traditional to contemporary. When time came for us to go totally contemporary, there were no repercussions from our members.

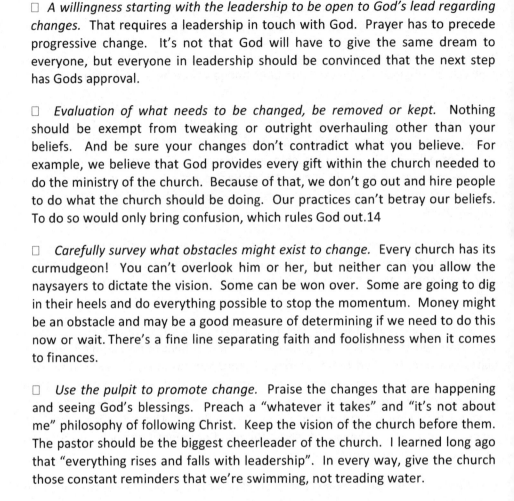

☐ *A willingness starting with the leadership to be open to God's lead regarding changes.* That requires a leadership in touch with God. Prayer has to precede progressive change. It's not that God will have to give the same dream to everyone, but everyone in leadership should be convinced that the next step has Gods approval.

☐ *Evaluation of what needs to be changed, be removed or kept.* Nothing should be exempt from tweaking or outright overhauling other than your beliefs. And be sure your changes don't contradict what you believe. For example, we believe that God provides every gift within the church needed to do the ministry of the church. Because of that, we don't go out and hire people to do what the church should be doing. Our practices can't betray our beliefs. To do so would only bring confusion, which rules God out.14

☐ *Carefully survey what obstacles might exist to change.* Every church has its curmudgeon! You can't overlook him or her, but neither can you allow the naysayers to dictate the vision. Some can be won over. Some are going to dig in their heels and do everything possible to stop the momentum. Money might be an obstacle and may be a good measure of determining if we need to do this now or wait. There's a fine line separating faith and foolishness when it comes to finances.

☐ *Use the pulpit to promote change.* Praise the changes that are happening and seeing God's blessings. Preach a "whatever it takes" and "it's not about me" philosophy of following Christ. Keep the vision of the church before them. The pastor should be the biggest cheerleader of the church. I learned long ago that "everything rises and falls with leadership". In every way, give the church those constant reminders that we're swimming, not treading water.

Here's what I found to be true. When over a period of time - years, not weeks or months - a culture of change has been created and sustained, the changes that will make the most impact in bringing life, growth and health to a church will become increasingly easier to bring about. But it takes time, and it takes commitment from the replanted to stick with the stuff. When the church sees that, it will follow your lead.

Yet even with the plan of God in your hand, there will be those who oppose anything new. How you handle that is what's next.

---

14 1 Corinthians 14:33 NKJV

Chapter 10
ADVERSITY BUILDS SOLIDARITY

We all have heard, and some of us experienced, church battles that led to splits. I was a member of a church that had a business meeting to choose the carpet. Really. An hour of our time wasted over something a couple of people on the building committee could have done if empowered to do so. Fortunately, it didn't divide us. But it could have!

Here's what I've learned. It's not necessarily the biggest changes that invoke the biggest fight.

In chapter 9, I told you about when we removed the large oak pulpit and "thrones" from the platform. By the way, it was a tiny platform. In its place, I used a wooden pedestal stand built years ago by one of the church craftsmen. What had taken three feet now consumed only 20 inches of space. I didn't ask anyone's permission. It was a decision of practicality. And I was the one using it, so shouldn't I have the freedom and power to replace it? I thought so.

So, I wasn't prepared when about a minute before the service was to begin, as I was placing my Bible and notes on the stand, that I looked up to see one of our senior sisters - a deacon's wife - coming down the aisle with a look on her face that wasn't screaming, "I love you, Pastor!" I had seen that same face on my mom when she was about to grab my ear!

As she got right up to the front, with incredulity oozing from her eyes, she said, "What have you done with MY pulpit?" With less than a minute, I didn't have the time to sit down with her, hold her hand and ask for her forgiveness. I just looked at her with equal incredulity and said, "Your pulpit?" Had I been a bit quicker on my feet, I would have offered to help load her pulpit in the back of her husband's pickup so she could take it home where it belonged. But, I didn't.

That pulpit never made its way back to the platform. It didn't become the start of a church fight, although she could have taken it there. She and her deacon husband didn't stay around much longer, however.

Years ago, I visited a pastor friend at a very old, traditional church in our area. Very old. Nearly 300 years old. He was facing a power play in the church, and I stopped by to give him some encouragement. Standing in the church's otherwise empty "sanctuary", our conversation was punctuated by the ticking of a pendulum clock hanging on the back wall. "That would drive me nuts," I said. "Why don't you take it down, and if you need a clock, put one up that is silent?"

You can guess his answer. The clock had been put up by somebody's grandfather way back when, and if it was removed, there would surely be an uproar. And an uproar over a clock was the last thing he needed. Never mind the ticking could be heard by everyone and had to be a distraction for some.

Upsetting the applecart of tradition isn't something new. Jesus' greatest opponents, the Pharisees, saw His new ideas as destroying their traditions. The Gospels record their disdain at His disciples for not washing their hands before eating. He then raked them over the coals for totally missing the point.

What causes big opposition, the kind that will give you heartburn and keep you lying awake at night? I've discovered a few causes.

☐ *A lack of understanding.* It's not necessarily that they don't know the new vision. The pastor may have effectively articulated it, and it's been an easy to remember phrase. They just don't understand why it needs to change and what was wrong with the way things were. They're not evil preacher-haters. They just don't get it. And the challenge for every replanter is to do his best to help them (not make them) understand. I say not make them because some simply will choose not to grasp it. The next point perhaps explains why.

☐ *The fear of the unknown.* We're afraid of what we don't understand. Another of my favorite movies is Remember the Titans. Part of the story is the friendship that evolves between two team captains, one white and the other black. Initially, they were enemies simply because of their racial differences. But, as the story progresses, they learn to become the best of friends. When the white player is paralyzed in an auto accident, he only wants one person to visit him in his hospital room: his black best friend. He looks at him and says, "I was afraid of you, Julius. I only saw what I was afraid of, and now I know I was only hating my brother."

In the church, Christian people can allow their fear of what they don't understand to become hate. And that's an ugly thing among the people of God.

☐ *The loss of power, whether real or perceived.* Typical of comatose churches is the power yielded by the few. They control who is nominated for positions and committees. And the powerful don't necessarily have to hold office in the church. They may be the "big givers" or the descendants of the families that started the church. And in all those generations, nothing has changed, and they like it like that. When Pastor Replant comes along, and new members are added and want to serve, the "old guard" often stiffens against them.

Our new bylaws put the leadership of the church into the hands of a body of pastors. So much of what had been decided in church business meetings would now be determined by the pastors, who would be plural in number. At the time, we had one pastor and three deacons. I   personally had trained them about the biblical model of deacons being the servants of the church. Never during that time did they handle the budget or financial decisions. But, when they realized that greater authority over church matters would be handled by the pastors, two of the three - good men who had come to the church after me - resigned. Their perceived power was lost. One came back but was never the same and left for good a few years later.

☐ *Believing they own something that belongs to the Lord.* This is the twin of the loss of control. It's the "I was here before you came, and I'll be here when you leave" mentality. Often, you'll see this in rural congregations when a prominent family or two rules the roost. They're the ones who donated the clock!

☐ *A different vision.* In reality, most dying churches have no vision other than keeping things the way they've always been. The air has been long gone from their balloon. But even though vision might not be articulated as such, it is usually heard from the pulpit. Before taking the pastorate, I heard these two visionary statements.

"We're here to give the summer tourists a place to go to church." Our church is in a resort/vacation mecca, with our county population swelling from 35,000 to 250,000. Believe it or not, some folks on vacation want to go to church. So, the vision was simple: We'll hang on and try to maintain in the off-season in order to provide a place to worship and hear God's Word in the summer.

A replant meant that had to change. The church, if it was to reach out to the communities around it, had to put the local population as the priority. We still love our vacation worshipers, but they're icing on the cake.

The second visionary statement was, "We'll never sing a song that isn't in the Baptist Hymnal". I'm not going to spend much time with that one. There are plenty of books written about the "worship wars" churches experience. But that statement says much about vision, and the vision it expresses is, "We are locked in to the past musically. Nothing worth singing to God has been written in the Christian world since the last century." Short-sighted vision leads to a dead-end road quickly.

    ☐ *An evil heart.* You almost hate to admit it. We never want to think a believer can work against the church. Then again, only the naive believe that every church roll is comprised 100% of believers. But, sometimes, the devil just plants evil-doers in the church or corrupts the minds of the saints. They may not start out that way; in fact, the ones who profess to be your greatest supporters might become the greatest opposition to bringing life back into the church.

Paul had a man named Alexander who was such a person. Alexander the coppersmith did great harm to me. The Lord will repay him according to his works. Watch out for him yourself, because he strongly opposed our words.15 Likely, this man was the same Alexander who teamed up with Philteus in Ephesus and taught false doctrine. As a result, Paul excommunicated him from the Ephesian church.16 Apparently, however, this Alexander still had influence over some in the church. Thus, the warning to Timothy in the second letter.

Satan is the enemy of the church, and his worst nightmare is for a sleeping, dying church to be revived. So, he seeks those within the church who will turn against the leaders trying to bring about change. They'll often couch their opposition with scripture, usually taken out of context, as a reinforcement of their behavior.

The best defense against opposition is the Great Commission. A church that is beginning to win new converts and disciple them is a formidable force. Those newly won by the Gospel are going to be loyal to the replanters vision and will

---

[15] 2 Timothy 3:14-15

[16] 1 Timothy 1:20

stand up to opposition. They'll hold to the "dance with the one who brung you" axiom.

An older couple joined our church fairly early into my pastorate. I don't recall exactly how they found us, but they were enthusiastic about being part of a growing congregation. However, our new bylaws, which turned greater decision-making authority over to the church's pastors, gave them great concern. In their words, we were no longer going to operate church "business" by Roberts' Rules of Order. And, of course, they were right, but they saw it as almost an unbiblical move. I received a phone call from her, asking, "What has happened to MY church?"

We set up a time to meet, and soon I was visiting in their home. That evening, I did my best to convince them that we were moving closer to the biblical model, not farther away from it, and that parliamentary procedure just couldn't be found in the New Testament church. Rather than leave the church, they chose to stay. But never again were they as active as before, becoming Sunday attenders and giving up their ministry positions.

The following year, at a banquet of some sort, I was surprised to see them present. I welcomed them and even sat beside them. He looked around the room, and with a look of surprise said, "I don't know anyone here". Of course, had he and his wife been faithful, had they found ways to serve, and had they joined a small group, they would have seen a room filled with their friends. But, they gave that all that up as they held on to their spirit of opposition. They didn't last much longer with us. They had been big givers. Yet it was better for them to leave than to remain disgruntled. And God brought in new members to take up whatever slack they left.

I've discovered that when the opposition attacks, the faithful lock arms and build a fortress around the protection of the vision and the visionary. Sometimes, circling the wagons bonds you together and makes the church stronger.

Chapter 11
A GREAT COMMISSION VISION

The history of Nags Head Church, like most of our denomination's congregations, is found in the reading of the minutes of church business meetings. Ever since its inception, the church teetered constantly on the brink financially. A representative from the Baptist State Convention visited in 1960 to make an evaluation and noted that it was due to the "blue-collar" status of its members and a seasonal income. Most of the church were fishermen, carpenters and a few cottage court owners. Pastors were always bi-vocational, which isn't unusual in a church of less than 100 in what at that time was considered a "rural" environment.

The desire to have a full-time pastor was always there, just never within reach. Once, in the early 1980's, they "stepped out on faith" to pay the pastor a full-time salary, only to totally deplete the funds in a matter of months. One answer to finding money to sustain the church's ministries was to cut out missions giving. That was short-lived, however. The pastor went back to being bi-vocational, and the church resumed giving to missions.

It's not uncommon for struggling churches to look at ways to save money. Churches are no different than households when it comes to budget deficits. We can't spend what we don't have. So, we find ways to cut back. In larger churches, it might mean cutting back staff either to part-time or cutting positions out altogether. But, and to our shame, the first cuts are too often to missions. We rationalize that other churches will cover the losses. In a denomination as large as ours, and with a pretty amazing system called the Cooperative Program, a tiny church dropping its annual giving of a couple of thousand, or even a few hundred dollars, won't put a large dent in the bucket. In non-denominational or independent churches, it might mean that the missionary must work a bit harder during "furlough" to raise needed funds.

And after all, we find biblical reason. God owns the cattle on a thousand hills, right? He promised the missionary Paul that He would "supply all his needs" (and the context is his financial support as a missionary/evangelist). Surely, God doesn't want our church at home to suffer loss. So, cutting back or cutting out missions giving, as the discussion goes around the table, is our best bet. Somehow, that promise to Paul must not apply to financially strapped churches.

One sign a church is declining is her focus becomes gradually inward. That's especially true when survival mode sets in. Of course, the ramifications of that change are many and always negative. And before long, a congregation sees itself as being solely about itself. While there may be a spirit of "love" and fellowship, an ingrown fellowship will soon begin picking itself apart. Gossip, jealousy, apathy and an overall critical spirit will grow from it. Why? Because that's not how Christ designed us. So, it's no surprise that an "Us four and no more" attitude can be prevalent in a church in need of a replant.

Because **a church's budget reflects its vision**, our first budget in our replanting years required a greater, not lesser, commitment to missions. In the same business meeting when the previous pastor graciously gave his resignation and asked the church to give me the call to move from being the interim pastor to being their shepherd, another motion was put to the floor by one of our newer members. I'll paraphrase his words. "If we're going to grow, we need to have a full-time pastor to lead us. So, I make the motion that we put together a budget for the remainder of the fiscal year [5 months] that will do just that." Interestingly, the church had not had a budget for probably decades. Operating on a shoestring, whenever the need arose to spend money, they had a business meeting and either approved or denied it.

Since January, the offerings had tripled for two reasons. First, the church began to grow. Second, with spring time comes a new season of tourism and prosperity. So, his motion that we should provide a full-time salary wasn't totally out of left field. The growth, the baptisms and the few new ministries and little improvements that had been started gave hope to a brighter future. But, before the motion could be put to a vote, I inserted a stipulation that with this new budget would be a commitment that no less than 10% of the budget be sent out to missions. I explained to them that God would bless us as we blessed missions, and that we should see it as a tithe (we are Baptists!) back to God. They wholeheartedly agreed!

Within a short time - a couple of weeks as I recall - a 5-month budget was prepared by an elected committee and our line items for missions were at the top. Twenty-seven years later, I can give God the glory that our giving to missions has always exceeded a tithe (typically around 15%), and that it remains the first section of our annual budget. There have been some tough financial years, especially as we saw a recession in our country's economy. And we have made some tough decisions in finding ways to tighten our belt. But, we have held firm on our giving to missions.

There came an opportunity to purchase more adjacent property that came available to us. We wondered how we could afford it. Property in our area, a resort community with little available land, is very expensive. A deacon suggested to me that if we cut back on our missions giving, it would make the purchase easier. Once again, I reminded him of our conviction that if we expected God's blessing on our finances, we had to take care of those sent out to do the work of the Great Commission abroad. This particular fellow was one who left the church over control of the money. But God has met our needs.

The Great Commission is the basis for who we are as a church. Christ left us with these words to, *Go into all the world and make disciples*[17]. But is that commitment solely financial? The simple way out, may I say, the first step for a church is to give funds to support missions. In replanting, that is probably where you must start in getting the church to look outward. And over the years, our giving has extended to an ever-increasing outreach locally to our community. The white fields ready-to-harvest are not only across the ocean. They're across the street and across town. They're right here.

God has allowed us to do some creative things within our local culture to reach out with the Gospel. For nearly 20 years now, we've held surf camps in the summer for youth. Why? There are lots of surfers in our church! And these dedicated men and women use surfing to have an opportunity to share the good news of salvation with kids.

For several years, we did a "Trunk or Treat" on Halloween. The numbers started with less than 100 and grew to over 2,000 in attendance. It was *the* big event in our area! School supplies were provided freely to needy kids in Operation Backpack. We support our local food pantry and crisis pregnancy center. Our newest local mission venture is helping our foster parenting community. And all are staffed with volunteers from the church. When they get personally involved in missions, they also are willing to invest financially in missions. It's not complicated.

---

[17] Matthew 28:19

The Lord has also opened many doors to us to send teams, both here in the US and abroad to assist missions' efforts. In 1991, it was unheard of in our church that someone from our church might actually be sent. That door continues to open wider, and our goal is to see every one of our partners (our word for members) have the opportunity to go and serve churches elsewhere. Perhaps the one thing that (if I can say this the right way) I am most proud of is that from our church, we have had six families go off into full-time missions. My prayer is that more will follow.

Getting the church to look beyond itself is about casting vision. And re-casting vision, over and over again. As we dedicated our new facility a few years ago, the vision was cast that it would primarily be a "launch pad for missions". We remind parents that God might call their children to go, and that they should be supportive of that calling, even exposing them to the possibility as they grow up. Missionaries frequently visit us and personally update the church on how they are doing.

If I could point to the top three reasons God has revived the church, one would be our emphasis on missions and outreach. It's about having a Great Commission vision.

Chapter 12
INVEST IN MEN!

Godly men are the backbone of a healthy church.

At the risk of being politically incorrect, let me go there.

Don't get me wrong. If it was not for godly women, most churches don't stand a chance. But, sad to say, the men are often more than willing to let the ladies take the lead while they sit in the background. Look around your church this Sunday. Are there more adult males or females?

Lots of reasons exist for the disparity between men and women. Some, however may be more excuses than reasons. Women tend to be more sensitive to the things of God. They're typically more open to sharing the particulars of their journey than are men who tend to be more private. It's easier to find women ready and willing to serve, especially in children's ministries, than it is men, but that may also be a more "natural" fit for them.

But, if a church is going to not only reach men but follow the Scriptures, there must be an intentional effort at building up the faith in her men. And the fact is that's better accomplished when men can follow other men as examples. We guys tend to struggle with the idea of women - even godly women - teaching us how to be spiritually healthy males.

One of my favorite passages along these lines is 2 Timothy 2:2. Writing to one of his younger proteges, Paul taught Timothy to invest in building up men in the Ephesian church. This was a church that, at the time, had a longer-than-most history, having been planted, it appears, by the trip of Apollos, Priscilla and Aquila, at the close of Paul's second missionary journey. It was during his third journey that Paul arrived in Ephesus, gathered the disciples there and stayed at least three years, being with them longer than with any other church in Asia

Minor or Europe.[18]   Later, he would send Timothy to Ephesus to dispel false doctrines being taught there and to "strongly engage in battle" [19].

While I doubt it can be said that Timothy's role in Ephesus was as a replanter, it had some similarities as this younger man would need to make some corrections in the direction, leadership and teaching of the church. It was in his second letter to Timothy that Paul would say, *And what you have heard from me in the presence of many witnesses, commit to faithful men who will be able to teach others also.*[20] It seemed that Paul recognized the necessity of Timothy identifying faithful men in the church and investing in them for the future of the church.

Who were these men? We're not given their names, but some may have been elders (pastors) already in the church. Paul had addressed these men as he told them goodbye after spending three years himself teaching them. The story is found in Acts 20 beginning in verse 17. And in his farewell to them, he actually warned them that, from among their group, false teachers would arise and divide the church. But, some does not mean all. So, it could be that Timothy would continue what Paul had begun with those who were counted as "faithful". Paul, in his first letter to Timothy, had instructed him not to allow any to "despise" his being younger than the elders of the church, giving support to the elders being among those Timothy would instruct.

There is also no reason to doubt that among the faithful men would be newer converts who perhaps did not have the advantage of sitting under Paul's teaching. Faithful does not mean mature in years. Who hasn't seen how younger believers tend to put the older to shame when it comes to faithfulness? So, Timothy, find faithful men and disciple them, invest in them, allow them to catch the vision and to be grounded in sound doctrine.

Even in dying churches, there is likely a remnant of the faithful. It seems odd that they haven't left the sinking ship for a church that is growing and thriving. Sometimes, there isn't another church like that in the area. That's the primary reason my family traveled an hour and a half one way each Sunday. I was blessed to find that, at Nags Head, there were the faithful who were clinging to the life that remained. They were not necessarily mature Christians, but they loved the Lord and their church. And they became the core of the renewal. I focused on the men, with the exception of one, all older than me.

---

[18] Acts 20:31

[19] 1 Timothy 1:3-4,18

[20] 2 Timothy 2:2

There were three ways we rallied and built up the men in the church.

☐ *We spent time together in the Word.* Our church had only one adult Sunday school class. So, to get the men together, we began an early morning Bible study that met in a local restaurant. Once a week, we would gather and spend time together in the Scriptures. This was a small group, just a handful at most. So those who were working could meet with us, we met before work. For some, this might have been the first "out of church" Christian experience. And that's a building block to greater things for them.

☐ *We spent time together in fellowship.* Once a month, a larger group of guys met on Saturday mornings for a prayer breakfast. All men were welcome, including boys and youth. At times, we met at the church where a couple of the men would prepare the breakfast for us. My son, who is now approaching middle-age, still remembers that "Mr. Harry" made the best scrambled eggs he's ever eaten! At times, we would go to a restaurant where we might be able to get a private room. And while we ate, we would talk, tell jokes, laugh and just enjoy being together.

I'd ask one of the men in advance to share his faith story - how he came to know the Lord and what God might be doing in his life at that time. Then, we'd pray together. Those who would prayed aloud. Those not yet there in their walk would pray silently and listen to others pray. It was a great way for the men to know that none of us are alone or on our own as we journey together. Those were some of the best times ever.

☐ *We spent time together serving.* Lots of men are handy. Those who aren't wish we were! But men like doing stuff with our hands and with tools. Fortunately, there were lots of projects to be done at the church. Some were outside, making repairs to rotting wood, tearing down a dilapidated church sign and putting up a new one, and pulling cactus! Our property, over years of neglect, had been overrun with little cactus. So, with shovels, spades and leather work gloves, we would spend a number of Saturdays (often after the prayer breakfast) digging up the cactus. And all the while we served together, we grew to know one another and become closer as men.

Those were simple ways of building into the lives of the men. Being personally involved in all of them, they got a better understanding of their pastor and of the vision God had given me for the church. And most of them gladly gave their support and wanted to see the church move forward in our mission to reach our community and the world.

Did every man join in the Bible studies, the breakfasts or the service projects? No. Not every man is "faithful". Don't fret over those who don't get involved. Instead, be thankful for those who, even though they may be few, do get involved and pour into them.

We need godly men to rise up and take on leadership roles within the church. We need them to shoulder the tough decisions that sometimes must be made. From the start, I began to pull men together and built relationships with them, and they with one another. There would be challenges ahead, and I would be counting on these guys to take us through them. Men want to lead their homes. They want to make a difference in their church.

They just need a Timothy to rally the troops and teach them how to do it.

Chapter 13
TURNING SACRED COWS INTO STEAK

I want to sing with Tevyeh in *"Fiddler on the Roof"*. "Tradition, tradition!"

Traditions, most of them, don't do the church any good when it comes to being relevant in an ever-changing culture that we're called to reach. And it's when those traditions morph over time (and they will) into non-negotiable practices reaching the status of scripture that the church is in need of life support. Something that may have started as new and improved, if not regularly evaluated and, more importantly, compared with Scripture, will in a couple of generations become religion.

A few short years into my pastorate, and not too long after our change in polity and structure, I heard this statement in a meeting with two deacons. "I don't care what the Bible says...!" For those who know me, you know that was like a slap in my face and was nothing less than heresy. It wasn't like these two men hadn't sat under Bible teaching for a few years. They had. And it wasn't as though we had not gone together through the biblical concept of deaconship. We had. But, for these two older gentlemen, years of tradition prior to their coming to our church had not been erased and was raising its head in defiance.

Before the meeting was over, they both handed me their pre-written letters of resignation as deacons of the church. So, really, whatever I had to say, whatever Scripture I read, was met with deaf ears. Their preconceived grasp (by virtue of another church's tradition) of church structure and leadership had never been buried. It had just been put away in a closet somewhere. The fact that a younger man, old enough to be their son and who had served with them as deacons, had recently moved out of that office and was now serving with me as a pastor probably was giving them indigestion as well.

In replanting a tradition-bound church, **it may be necessary to, at the very least, tweak the church's structure, if not do a total overhaul.** The reason is that its system for decision making has either been long ignored, or it can't be found in Scripture. Ours is and has always been a Southern Baptist Church, and, from its inception in the 1950's, had always had a typical, traditional (at least since the years after the Civil War) Baptist polity. But, of course, no one alive today can remember how we processed decisions and formulated vision or chose pastors before the latter 19th century. So, how we did things in 1990 was all anyone knew, so it must have been "how we've always done it".

When I preached that first Sunday night series "God's Work God's Way", I had stressed the importance of our constantly evaluating ourselves as a church by looking in the Book. The first Sunday morning I preached as their interim-pastor, I made this statement, "Before we make any decisions as a church, our first question ought to be, 'What does the Bible say?'" That ministry philosophy was laying a foundation, a strong foundation, that would serve us well later as we dismantled and then rebuilt our structure. Whenever I had the opportunity, I reminded them of our belief in the Reformation cry of *Sola Scriptura*.

You may not follow the same path we took. You may already have in place the right flow chart. It might be that you've discovered not everyone elected or chosen (however your church does things) was not exactly qualified to serve there. How many boards are chosen by popularity or ability to give or because of business acumen? For how many is being elected to the board an ego-builder rather than a step of humility? Is the position seen as one of power or one of servant-leadership?

Of course, you can't come in and in the first month announce, "We're about to make some sweeping changes in our leadership!". Well, you can make that announcement, but I hope you haven't already unpacked your boxes and set up your office. Be sure you read chapter 8 on Earning Trust. Changes like that take time and with that time comes credibility. They have to know you're not going to shake everything up then walk away.

So, let me say this. And this is especially for younger, fresh out of college or seminary pastors. If you view this dying church as a place for you to hit a home run and then leave, don't even try to change everything. All you'll do is hasten their death. Churches are not stepping stones for dreamy-eyed, wannabe preacher super-stars.

I needed to get that off my chest. Thanks!

Without trying to convert anyone to my beliefs about leadership in the church, you should know my context in order to understand our process. As I understand

Scripture, deacons are seen as servants to the church. Because of the language used in Acts 6, especially verse 3, I take it that these seven Greek Christian Jews were at the least the prototype for the deacons. Their one and only job at the time was to care for the Greek-speaking widows in the church, which would free the Apostles/pastors to focus on prayer and teaching. Paul wrote to Timothy, as he outlined the qualifications for deacons, that those who serve the church well in that role, "acquire a good standing for themselves". Good deacons are worth their weight in gold and should be given respect for their service. But, they are never seen as the ruling board to which a pastor answers.

In every church Paul planted (Acts 14:23), he took the model of the Jerusalem church and installed elders (or pastors). The elders in Ephesus were told by Paul that they had been appointed (that's different than elected, right?) by the Holy Spirit to their role and were to shepherd, lead and manage God's flock. Always in Scripture a plurality of elders/pastors is seen in the local church.

Although Nags Head gave more authority to its pastor than most Baptist churches, the deacons served primarily as a sounding board to the pastor, and every decision made was done so in a church business meeting and by a democratic vote. Finding none of that in the biblical model, my goal from the onset was to restructure how the church was led. And for us, that meant dismantling tradition.

Bob and Steve were two spiritually mature men who came into the church after me. As the church began to know them, it was clear they were respected for their walk with the Lord, for the stability of their marriages, for their longevity in the faith and for their knowledge of the Word. One had moved to the area from a church with elders. The other had not. God impressed on me that these two men had the potential to be our first elders. So, more than a year before I taught a series on church leadership and then put the ball in motion to replace the old with the new, I began to meet regularly with them individually and then together, studying the Word and seeing if they were up to the task. Thankfully, they were.

When that year was up, I then taught a series on Sunday morning on biblical church leadership, showing from the Scriptures the relationships between pastors, deacons and the church. At the end of the five-week series, I invited everyone to come back that evening for a Q and A session on what we had covered. I was hoping for a particular question to be asked, and thankfully, it was! "If this is what the Bible says, why aren't we doing it?" I could see lots of heads nodding.

To shorten the story, I proposed a process by which we would change our polity. A new Constitution and By-laws committee would be formed with the task of coming up with one that reflected the change. Interestingly enough, no committees were mentioned in the new version, and to this day, the word "committee" is taboo in our church! Instead, we have lots of ministry teams which are empowered to do the ministry.

The church was asked to appoint Steve and Bob as "provisional" elders, serving with me (not under me) over the next nine months so that the church could see how a team of pastors worked. The church heartily agreed on those two men. We began to meet monthly to pray for and manage the affairs of the church. Church "business meetings" became known as church "conferences" and consisted primarily of hearing reports from the elders. The only votes taken were those requiring action other than what might be routine. Major financial actions, like buying property or taking a loan to do so, required congregational approval. So would the annual budget. As you can imagine, few votes were taken. And that's a good thing because all a vote does is to require a choice which too often shows division. Church conferences became pep rallies, not debates.

The Constitution/By-laws took several months to draw up. Thankfully, there were other churches that had already gone through the same transition and were willing to share with us. Included in the Constitution is our church's Statement of Faith, spelling out our beliefs. Once the document was completed, it was distributed. Community meetings in homes were arranged where everyone was invited to come and ask questions and give input. Doing this in advance enabled the final decision to be overwhelmingly positive and without debate. Finally, at our annual church conference the new structure, including the Constitution and Bylaws were adopted, a new budget approved, and two new elders were approved and soon would be ordained.

Changing a well-seated tradition will not please everyone. Some said we were becoming Presbyterians! But, it was, in hind-sight, the best change we ever made for lots of reasons. It was one of two or three major transitions we would make that were like breathing a deep breath after holding it for too long of a time.

Here's what I learned:

☐ *Have a firm grasp on your ecclesiology from the start.* If your change is going to be anything like ours, you need to know exactly what you believe before you start trying to change anyone else's beliefs.

☐ *Expect some fierce battles over traditions that are dearly held,* even though they are not healthy. You may be the best teacher/communicator in the world. But some people will resist any change. And they'll be willing to attempt to mount support against you. If you don't have a good prayer life, you will need one!

☐ *Find your faithful core and start with them.* Build a team. And you don't need to announce the vision at once in totality to everyone! That's not being sneaky. It's being as wise as a serpent and harmless as a dove.

☐ *Establish a biblical or practical basis for replacing the tradition.* Not everything needs a biblical mandate. When we moved Sunday school to Sunday night, it wasn't because "the Bible says to do it". It was because we needed the time and space on Sunday morning to accommodate another worship gathering. Some will be shocked to hear that Sunday school isn't found in the Bible!

☐ I'll say it once more: *Do not rush.* God has a time and a place for everything. Start fast, don't last. If you're in it for the long haul, you're not in a sprint but a marathon.

In replanting, you'll find you'll be going where angels fear to tread when it's time to kill the sacred cows of counter-productive traditions.

Chapter 14
THE DOOR SWINGS BOTH WAYS

If you've ever replanted a plant from one pot to another, you know you're going to have to dig in the dirt and get some soil under your nails. This is where the replanters' hands get muddy. In every church, whether it is an established congregation doing well, a new plant or a replant, people are going to leave and either migrate to another church or, as often is the case, start something new. It is inevitable. And, depending on the leadership's personality and strength, some may even be asked to leave.

Church exits on the surface seem to be contrary to Christ's prayer in John 17, when He said to His Father, *I pray not only for these, but also for those who believe in Me through their message.*

May they all be one, as You, Father, are in Me and I am in You. May they also be one in Us,

so the world may believe You sent Me.[21] Oneness, unity of being and purpose was and is Christ's plan and design for His body. And I suppose that were we all fully surrendered to His will, church problems would be resolved with everyone intact and joyfully moving forward together. But, that's not reality, is it?

One of our earliest exits involved the organist. (Why is it that musicians seem to be in the middle of so many church troubles?) A year or two prior to my coming to the church, they found themselves without any musical accompaniment to their congregational singing. Those who had in prior years played either the piano or the organ (sometimes the accordion) had either left over church politics or had died. In a business meeting, which seems to be the time and place so many churches get into trouble, the pastor asked the congregation what they should do. Do we continue to sing sans instruments? Do we wait until God brings

---

[21] John 17:20-21

a new member who can play? Do we look outside and hire someone? They chose door number 3.

Allow me to insert a bit of my own ecclesiology here, and I know many disagree with what I'm about to say. I believe Christ builds the church. And in every church He builds, the Holy Spirit sovereignly places the member into the body[22]. Therefore, every church has every part necessary at the time to do the ministry of the church at that stage of its life. My conclusion, then, is that the church does not need to look outside of its membership to plug in holes, whether they be musicians or nursery workers. And -here it comes - if the church has been making disciples, they should be able to look no farther than their own congregation to find their next pastors! God's people either need to step up to the plate or patiently wait for the Spirit to provide their need through healthy growth. Sometimes, we're better off without than we are moving ahead of God.

Someone in the church knew of a man who played the organ. Although not a Baptist, he was the son of a minister of another (very different) denomination. And for payment, he was available. Soon, he was playing the organ, and much to the consternation of the pastor, pretty much taking over the service. And, he was quite the showman! He and the song leader (I mentioned him earlier) were often out of sync. On more than one occasion, the pastor confided in me that he didn't know what to do. The music had become a major embarrassment.

After my first Sunday, I had a meeting with the organist and the song leader and laid down some ground rules. First, I would select the songs to be sung. It was time to move beyond the same twelve or so songs. There would be no "special" (and that's a perfect word for what was happening) music unless it was first auditioned before me and given my approval. None. It was very apparent in that meeting that the air was let out of the balloons. But my concern was about our worship services being orderly and as good as we could make them than hurting feelings. Guests don't return to poorly planned church. So, the bar was raised that first week.

That lasted about a month. Then, on a Sunday at 10:50, ten minutes before we were to begin the service, our organist was nowhere to be found, and no one had heard from him. So, with our new telephone, I called him. "I'm not feeling well", he told me. "That's OK", I said, "Get well." That he hadn't bothered to call anyone was telling.

---

[22] 1 Corinthians 12

New to the church was Bob (who later became an elder), and I knew that he was proficient on the piano. "Bob, we're in need of a pianist this morning. Could you fill in?" The next two weeks, the other guy was ill. On that third Sunday, he did call, and I told him not to worry, we had someone else who was playing now. "If you have someone else, then that's OK with me." Thus ended his stint as our organist. And it saved us $50 a week!

Two other men in this tiny congregation had been ordained somewhere in their pasts, and when the pastor began to talk of retirement, they each saw themselves as likely successors. The rest of the church didn't share their ambitions, however. When it became clear that wasn't going to happen (and honestly for good reasons), they left on their own volition to go to other local churches.

God knows who your church needs. Let Him bring the right person in to fill a need, if indeed it is one. Someone has said that the human voice is the most beautiful instrument ever created. If that's all you've got on Sunday, make a joyful noise!

And, if that's true...

God knows who your church doesn't need. The temptation in seeing life brought back into a dying church is to take in all comers. Resist that temptation! From what I've seen in the evangelical culture here in the United States, there is a failure on the part of churches and their leadership to expect commitments from members. Some have called it a "consumer" church mentality, where it's all about what the church can do for them. You don't need consumers.

Other exits were not so simple or painless. Some are those you have counted on and have discipled. But they never get the vision, or if they get it, they don't buy into it. Many of those are people who transfer in when they hear the church has a new (and in our case, young) pastor. They're not happy where they are - usually they've got a beef with the pastor. You can count on this: 90% of the time, they'll bring that baggage with them, and eventually they'll continue grinding that axe on the new pastor's hide. And don't be surprised if their reasons for leaving put all the guilt on the pastor and church leadership.

Then, there are those who come in joyfully, with a seemingly wonderful testimony, and a resume that is just what you need. They've served elsewhere in this ministry and that, been a deacon, and maybe even have a Bible college diploma somewhere. But, not too far down the road. you start hearing, "At my old church, we did it *this* way." Or, "I appreciate the church's vision, but I'd rather we focus on this instead."

The danger these folks present is that in the months or years perhaps that they've been attending or been members, they've gained a "following". It may be a Sunday school class or a small group. And although they may truly be Christian people, if they don't buy into the vision, they don't need to stay. Someone (the pastor with another respected leader) needs to have "the talk" with him or her or them. Wish them well. Thank them for their support in the past. But if it isn't going to work, it isn't going to work.

Those exits are hardest to overcome because often those they've influenced and who don't see the conflicts will go with them. That happened here once. We lost an entire small group of about a dozen adults - good people - who were led to believe by a dominant non-member that the direction of the church was somehow less than biblical. In his words, we had "lost our spiritual compass". Really for him, the issue was our music. When he was told by one of our elders not to come back to church, the entire group but for one younger couple went elsewhere as well. That was not our intention, but it was the risk we had to take. Some good people were lost, and that hurts.

Brace yourself. **The exit door might swing more often for a while than the entrance.** But, for the sake of the church, you have to let them go. We learned some painful, but invaluable, lessons from those experiences and have since put some safeguards in place to try and prevent repetition.

Paul, in 1 Corinthians 12, describes the church as a body, with *feet, hands, ears, eyes*, and so forth. What a great way to explain how the church works together as one. I want to add this to the "body" description. Every body now and then needs a cleansing. Prune juice does a body good. Don't make me go further with this! You get my drift.

Although that all sounds negative, it isn't. But, let me finish with a positive suggestion.

Ours is a transient community. A growing proportion of our population are retirees. Another large proportion are younger families, looking to live the good life at the beach. As a result, we get a lot of people new to our area who are looking for a new church home. That's exciting! When I meet them, I always ask, "How did you find our church?", looking for their reasons for showing up with us on a Sunday. The #1 answer for new residents is, "Your website". That's exciting! Just behind that would be that someone from the church or someone they know at work, etc. either attends our church or has heard good things about it. That's extra exciting. And they'll often say something to the effect, "This church is just like our church back home."

Well, maybe. Maybe not. There may be similar music, preaching style, small groups, etc. Usually newcomers from other locales are looking for similar. We're glad they found us. But they need to know more about us before saying "I do". Church membership is very much like a marriage, isn't it? And if they say, "We're Baptists, and so are you", I know there are some differences.

The best way to explain to those checking you out and considering membership bar none is to teach an introductory class that lays out who your church is. Call it a new members class, 101 (from the Purpose Driven Church paradigm), Discovering (your church name) Church, or whatever. But, have a class. And make taking that class a requirement for membership. This will save you a ton of heartache down the road. Here's why.

In the class, you teach a little church history (*your* church history, not the Reformation), your beliefs, your vision, purposes, mission, what to expect from the church and what the church will expect from them. You can do this in a couple of hours. It doesn't have to be weeks and weeks (like we used to do). Give them a snapshot but go through the things you want every member of your church not only to know, but to get and to agree with. Agreement is a big thing, isn't it? The opening chapter of the first church's history tells us they were *all of one accord.*[23] God asked Amos, *Can two walk together, unless they are agreed?*[24] There must be agreement on the things that matter.

In years of teaching the class, I have had some who take it and we never see them again. Something said in the class disagreed with them, so they decided to look elsewhere for a church home. Maybe they want something closer to their church back home. Maybe they don't like our structure. Who knows (unless they tell us). But, that's OK. I'd rather have them leave before they become members, than to leave a year later because they just didn't fit, or they didn't agree, or worse, stay and be contentious. And in the class, I explain to them that if they discover that we're probably not the church for them, let me know and I'll help them find that church.

What about those who are attending and haven't yet become Christians? One of the things I do in every class is explain the Gospel at the beginning of the class. And at the conclusion of that segment, I give an invitation to receive Christ right then and there. It's a great opportunity to evangelize. But, most seekers probably aren't going to take the class without first knowing they have the same kind of faith we talk about. Richard, however, was different.

---

[23] Acts 1:14 NKJV
[24] Amos 3:3 NKJV

Richard is a mature, retired guy in his 60's who was invited by one of our partners he met one day on the beach. So, he showed up on the following Sunday and sat on the front row! For the next year there he was, more faithful than a lot of our members. He would listen intently. He took notes. Bought a Bible. And every so often he would say, "I'm not there yet." When our Discovering Life in Christ class was announced, he signed up for it. And there he was for the class. No, he didn't accept Christ that day. But, he kept coming to church. And in the Lord's time, Richard raised his hand one Sunday saying he was putting his faith in Christ for his salvation. He was baptized soon after and took the next membership class. Now, he's in a small group, serves on a ministry team and is still sitting on the front row every Sunday.

As soon as you can, put together a class. At first, invite all the present members to take the class. It's actually part of our bylaws that the class is a requirement for membership, along with faith in Christ and believer's baptism. It's the easiest way to ensure that everyone starts out with you on the same page. Always assume that newcomers to the church need that introduction. Always.

So, what is the "prune juice"? Read on.

Chapter 15

RIGHT THE VISION AND MAKE IT PLAIN

Without playing too fast and loose with the Lord's words to the prophet Habakkuk, permit me to borrow His words. God was speaking to Habakkuk about His punishment on Israel by the hands of the Babylonians. The prophecy Habakkuk would give was to be written down on tablets, so it could easily be read and distributed among the people. They needed to know why bad times were ahead, but to also know that they would not be destroyed.

By the way, I meant for it to be "Right", not "Write". "Right" as in the verb, "correct". (Raise your hand if you thought it was a mistake.)

Vision for the replanted church cannot be minimized. It was vision that pretty much determined every step in our replant that has preceded this chapter. I'll confess, I didn't know much about "vision" as a 35-year-old who saw his past experiences in ministry as more failures than successes. As a college student, I heard Jerry Falwell (a great visionary) speak about it, but I thought being a "visionary" was something for the big-time pastors, not for those of us out in the hinter lands and rural areas.

I was wrong. God had given me a vision for Nags Head Church. So many days I had driven by the little white steeple-adorned chapel on my way to bang nails somewhere and thought God could do something greater there if this or that happened. Actually, that vision began as a seed more than a dozen years before I found myself being embraced as their new pastor.

Gail's dad owned a vacation/weekend getaway home in Kill Devil Hills, the town adjacent to Nags Head on the north. There are five small beach towns on the northern stretch of the Outer Banks. Without signs telling you you've left one and entered the next, you might think it is just a 25-mile-long town. He bought the home during our first year of marriage, for which we were grateful because it meant a free place to stay on vacation! And we took advantage of it.

Our first year of marriage, I was in local church youth ministry in Southern California. As my first year was coming to an end, we bought plane tickets and flew to the East Coast for two weeks. One week would be spent visiting our parents in Virginia. The other week was just us two at the beach. I've always been one to want to visit other churches when I'm away from home to see if I can learn something to take home. And I just think going to church to worship is the right thing for a Christian to do. But where would we go? The closest Baptist church to where we were staying was in Nags Head. So, on Sunday morning, there we were with a big summer crowd of other vacationers.

I don't remember what we sang. I think a blind girl came up and sang "I'd rather have Jesus than silver or gold." I don't remember a word of the sermon. But, I remember saying to Gail as we sat there, "This would be a cool place to be a pastor." When the week was over, we flew back to California, and I never imagined I would one day be pastoring that same church. It never crossed my mind for the next ten years. As far as I knew, I would be living out my life in California, and that was all right with me. But, God had other plans.

In those first few years at Nags Head Church, the vision God had for us was expressed in sermons, in sayings like "God's work God's way" and in always raising the bar to do church in a relevant way, better today than what we did yesterday. There was this vision. But it had never been written down.

There's something about writing things down, like goals and dreams and vision. When they're put down on paper, they become more real, more concrete. And when they're shared, suddenly there is an accountability to go by them.

Three of us, myself and our two other pastors (elders), were traveling to a conference of some sort in the Spring of 1996. Our replant had been in operation now for five years. God had done some amazing things raise the sinking ship. And we were counting on God for it to continue. There were still more lost people in our community than there were saved (still are!), so there was a future for us to sow seed and reap harvest. So, we came up with the idea of a Vision Statement, something that would, in concise form, serve as the rails on which our train would travel and stay on track. It was in that church van as we headed west through North Carolina that vision was written down.

None of us had ever done this before. I couldn't remember having ever been a part of a church that actually had such a statement. Sure, we had a statement of faith that spelled out what we believed as a church, but nothing that spelled out what we were to be. So, we thought back to the things about the church we had learned together, and the things we were striving to be in the years to come. Before the trip was done, we had come up with five points to our vision, all of them originating from scripture.

Someone might say, "The Bible is our vision statement", to which I say, "Amen!". But that's a big Book, and frankly, not all of it has to do with what a local church is to be. It's all relevant to our lives, but it doesn't all necessarily apply to where the church ought to be going. So, we pared the whole Bible (at least the relevant parts to the church) down to these five points.

1. Striving to be a **community** of united believers who care for and share with one another in the love of Christ. (*John 13:35*)

2. Committed to being **contemporary** in methods, yet **unchanging** in message. (*1 Corinthians 9:19-23*)

3. **Equipping** every member to maturity in their spiritual gifts for edification and evangelism, with a desire to **reach all** ages and social groups. (*Ephesians 4:11-16*)

4. **Celebrating** as a body the majesty of our God and the glories of His Son in meaningful worship. (*Psalm 95:1-7*)

5. Faithfully **supporting and promoting missions** through our giving, prayer and training; that from within our church God's call to missions will be accepted. (*Philippians 4:15-18*)

After we returned from the conference and had tweaked the wording to make sure it was simple and plain enough to follow, we printed it up and distributed it to the church. But we didn't simply want it to be the elders' vision for the church; we wanted it to be accepted as their vision. So, we did what Baptist churches do. We said that at our next quarterly church conference we would bring this statement up for a vote.

And you know how that turned out. All together in unity, we accepted it as God's plan for our church to keep on doing His work, His way. It's still our vision over 20 years later. It still guides our decisions and, thankfully, weeds out some things that we could be doing but don't because they don't fit within the vision. It keeps us on track when a lot of things come up that would derail or sidetrack us. God has used these words to keep us out of trouble on more than one occasion.

Here's one example. As my son was in his senior year of high school, a well-meaning older man with some financial resources suggested that the church establish a scholarship fund for young people from the church who were college bound. He pointed out that other churches in our area have such funds and each spring award them. First, I thanked him for thinking of my son and other young people. But can you imagine the can of worms that would have opened to start such a fund just as the pastor's son was going off to college? Our vision statement kept us out of that can. The answer to his question was easy to give. "It's not part of our vision to fund the college education of our youth. If you personally want to give a student a gift, that's totally up to you. But we won't funnel such gifts through the church. Other churches may do that, but we don't." I was well aware of how the IRS would have seen designated scholarships for my son.

It was not me telling him "No". It was the vision that he had supported all these years.

Would it have been better had we come up with this vision statement five years earlier? Probably not. I say that because a church should always be a work in progress. Had I proposed that we become a contemporary church, no one (probably including me) would have understood what that meant. But as the church matures and gets a grasp on who they are, there will come a time, perhaps sooner than five years, when such a written, adopted-by-the-congregation statement is needful.

Here are a few thoughts on putting your vision down on paper.

☐ *Get the vision from God.* What I mean by that is make it biblical. Be able to show your vision lines up with the Word. That means knowing what Jesus and the Apostles said and did in the context of the church.

☐ *Make it a team effort.* One of the greatest things about the church is the idea of community. For us, the team was our pastoral leadership, our elders. And honestly, who better to declare "this is the kind of church God wants us to be"? But if you don't have elders, pull together your most trusted, godly folks. I wouldn't make the group more than a handful; otherwise, you'll take forever to get it done.

☐ *Make it as concise as possible.* Actually, our five points might be longer than what most would recommend. But, for us, it says what needs to be said and no more. This is who we should be as a church. Now, we also have a mission statement that is very short and easily remembered. It is simply, "Love God. Love Others. Reach the World." That says what we're to do. And it's the second generation. Before that, it was "Reaching people to discover life in Christ". And I guess sometime in the future, the mission statement will have a new way of saying it.

☐ *Let the church adopt is as their own.* If they're with you, it's because they've already adopted the vision informally. But use its introduction as a time to promote unity and celebration. Maybe print it up on cards (there are really inexpensive ways to do that professionally) or on a document for them to keep. And eat some cake. Always find a reason to eat cake.

☐ *Stick with it.* If the truths expressed in your statement are biblical, then they are also eternal. You might find a need down the road to tweak the wording, but don't change the vision because (from the first point) you got it from God. That means before you settle on your vision statement, you need to be as sure as possible it is the finished product. But, you'll be like us. Before we wrote it down, it had been simmering in our hearts for several years.

☐ *Cast and recast often.* Hey, people forget! Judah forgot who they were to be because they "lost" the Law of Moses (the Pentateuch), and for years, it wasn't read. And during those years, under idolatrous kings, the people strayed away from God's vision for them. When it was found, Josiah the king read the entire Law to the people and they repented. It's not likely you'll physically lose your vision statement! But, if it isn't recast regularly, it could be forgotten.

That's not to say that it should become some kind of recited creed every Sunday. But find a way, pastor, to bring out its points, even if only one at a time in your sermons. If part of our vision fits with the context of a sermon, I'll remind the church that our vision is... and put it in their notes or up on the screen. Keep it before them. Maybe as you start the New Year, you can do a sermon on 'Our Vision' and preach it!

We didn't realize it at the time, but the Vision Statement was the point in our timeline when the U-turn of our church was complete. What had been "mostly dead" five years earlier was now alive and well. Life, however, must be sustained. Our ecclesiology tells us that the church is not an institution but a living organism. And that life continues to grow and learn and change. Now that God had guided us to new life, He knew we were ready to take more big steps in being the church He had envisioned 50 years earlier when a Sunday school began in a borrowed facility in a little beach village.

As long as the church continues to dream, make disciples and not be satisfied with the status quo, we'll remain healthy.

Chapter 16
CAN YOUR CHURCH COME BACK?

The day before I began to write this last chapter, this story appeared on my Facebook feed.

"'The right time: After 101 years, Florida Street Baptist to close its doors". According to Lifeway Research ten American churches are closing *each day*.

And then this popped up as I searched for the above story: "Another 60-plus Sears, Kmart stores to close."

One story is about a once thriving church in a large city that has been breathing its last for about two decades and are disbanding. It's a sad story, with video interviews of elderly and life-long members recounting the good old days of revivals and missions trips. At the end of that year, the church would no longer exist in any form, deeding its property to a private Christian school.

The other story is about the one-time retail giants Sears and K-Mart. Trying to stay alive, they are slashing the number of stores. For a number of years they have been circling the drain.

There are tremendous parallels between the church and the corporation that owns both Sears and K-Mart. And this same story is being repeated over and over as churches are closing their doors. I was a teenager in 1969 when the Florida Street church was running 1,000 in Sunday school, built a new education building and would be debt-free in 1971. It was a church described as being "ahead of the times" in many ways. But they came to the place where there were more pews than worshipers and no young people.

Likewise, the once giants of the retail world are closing doors of stores that have stood for decades. Online options for shopping have taken away the old model of going shopping.

Simply put, whether in church or in the business world, depending on the status quo will be the death knell. When we in leadership don't recognize the changes happening (more quickly than ever before) in our culture, we're putting the nails in the coffin. "The way we've always done it" is killing churches.

In many instances, the neighborhood around the church has changed over the generations. That is the story at Florida Street. As people like them moved out into the suburbs, new people moved in to the community. It doesn't take long for those moving, even just a few miles away, to start looking for a church closer to home. In the meantime, the church failed to find ways to reach out to their new community demographic, even if it meant planting a new church on their six acres of buildings and land that looked like the neighborhood.

The association with which my church affiliates is largely rural, with many churches over one and two hundred years old. When those churches were founded, their communities were very different. Travel to church was by horse drawn wagon. So, having a church close was important. As a result, there are many rural churches within five miles of another church just like them. But, the communities are no longer thriving. The young people go off to college and don't return. They don't want to farm, and there are no jobs at home. The result is small churches that once perhaps had 100 worshipers now have literally a handful meeting on Sundays.

And within a five to ten-mile radius are four or five such churches, all barely alive, only a few years from closing their doors. Suggest to those hanging on that perhaps they could merge with those other churches, and your suggestion will be quickly dismissed. Instead of four churches with 50 or 60 attenders total, they could be one congregation with that many. Empty pews would be filled. But, there are cemeteries. There are plaques on the walls with great-grandparents' names on them in that building. So, rather than move forward with a Kingdom mindset, they would rather be us four and no more until we die.

Church people can be among the most stubborn, short-sighted people in this world, especially when they see church property as belonging to them. The scary reality is that every church, mine and yours, can become Florida Street in just one generation. How can we do everything possible to prevent that?

- **As leaders, we must keep our eyes on the horizon and our ears to the ground.** Unless we keep up with the changes around us, we'll settle into a complacency that will doom us. When we began to replant in 1991, we started with a church that was doing church in the 1990's exactly how they had done it in the '50's. And the only ones who thought that was good were those who remembered the 1950's as the "good ol' days". Much is being said today about losing the millennial generation. We need to find out what makes them tick, and without compromising our message and beliefs, do what it takes to show them that Christianity something worth pursuing.

- **Cheerleading starts from the pulpit.** The pulpit is not just for preaching. Paul told Timothy to *give your attention to public reading, exhortation, and teaching.* (1 Timothy 4:13) In the pulpit there in Ephesus, Timothy was to do those things. "Exhortation" is from the Greek word *paraklesis,* which in its various forms is translated as "encourage" or "encouragement". And "encourage" means to "give courage". That's what cheerleading is: giving encouragement. The pastor needs to be the church's greatest cheerleader, leading the charge to continue to do whatever it takes to accomplish God's will. If the pastor fails to encourage and exhort, the church is bound to become satisfied with the "same ol' same ol'".

- **Get out there and learn!** Glean from those who are excelling in leadership, evangelism, transition, missions and whatever. There are great conferences being held in churches that simply want to share with you and me what they've learned. But here's the deal. We can tell ourselves that, "My church of 150 could never do what that church of 15,000 is doing, so why bother?". That's nothing short of pride. Every time I've been to a conference, whether it's at a big church or one not so big, I've come back with something we can do. And here's a tip: find a church in your region just a bit larger than yours that is hitting home runs and go learn from them. If the mega church conference overwhelms you, go to a conference at a church that is not so big and find out what they're doing.

- **Find visible ways to show the community that the church is alive.** Some folks who began to attend our church told me that they thought the church had closed down. When they would drive by during the week, they noticed the grass always needed to be cut. The sign was in disrepair. There were never any cars in the parking lot. It seemed nothing was happening. And they weren't far from the truth. The outside appearance of your buildings matters to the community. Creating a website that actually says something and is attractive says something. I confess. I visit church websites, and if they're hard to navigate or when they pop up I hear "Just a Closer Walk With Thee" (or something similar) playing, I go somewhere else. Get a pro to design a new logo and put it on everything. Tell the community what you're doing that's relevant and different through every media you can use. We tweet, Instagram and Facebook daily. What's great about those channels is that they're easily shared by your members. Last year, our kids' ministry had a float in the community Christmas Parade! Find ways to say to your community that good stuff is happening. Just be sure to do them with excellence.

- **Expect seasons and cycles.** There's an ebb and flow, a high and low tide in church life. You're not going to be in high gear all the time. And that's OK. There are seasons when we need to catch our collective breath before the next set of rideable waves comes back. And during those in between times, do some evaluation. Seek God's vision for the next season. And keep on encouraging. Until every soul has heard the Gospel, God is not finished with your church. There's more to do, and I'll bet He's called you to do it.

DEFINING TERMS (AS USED IN THIS BOOK)

Plant(ing) - a brand new church; establishing a new church.

Transitioning - moving a living (healthy or not) church from point A to point B, usually from a "traditional" model to a "contemporary" one.

Replanting - reviving a nearly dead church by gradually stripping away what hasn't worked, starting from the foundation and replacing it with new and healthy vision, structure and purposes. Leading a church to a second chance at life.

Vision - allow me to use Jerry Falwell's definition. He was one of the greatest visionaries I have known.

I believe vision is the basis for all successful ministry. To be a leader, one must be a visionary. He must certainly be able to see farther down the road than his peers. He must have some idea of where he is going, even if he doesn't know how he's going to get there. And those goals or visions that he sets out for himself become motivating factors and drive him out of complacency, out of a willingness to accept what is permanently. It brings him through hardships. It takes him out of present failure. It moves him on to capture the dream that God has put in his heart. It's also real vision, real spiritual vision that never allows you the luxury of discouragement. It never allows you to retreat. It never allows you to accept anything that is negative. - Jerry Falwell in an interview with Daniel Henderson. (Used by permission.)

ABOUT THE AUTHOR

Rick Lawrenson is the Lead Pastor of Nags Head Church in Nags Head, NC. He and his wife Gail have been married since 1977 and have 3 grown children and 4 grandkids. His education includes degrees from Liberty University and Liberty Baptist Theological Seminary. Rick authors a weekly column, *"Living on Purpose"* which appears in the Outer Banks Sentinel as well as an occasional blog post at beachpreach.com. He also serves the Nags Head Fire and Police departments and the Outer Banks Marine Corps League detachment as Chaplain.

Made in the USA
Middletown, DE
08 January 2022

58194206R00060